The Commercial Pilot's Licence

Anneli Christian-Phillips

WITHDRAWN FOR SALE

First published in 2013 by
The Crowood Press Ltd
Ramsbury, Marlborough
Wiltshire SN8 2HR

www.crowood.com

© Anneli Christian-Phillips 2013

All rights reserved. No part of this publication may be reproduced or transmitted in any form or by any means, electronic or mechanical, including photocopy, recording, or any information storage and retrieval system, without permission in writing from the publishers.

British Library Cataloguing-in-Publication Data
A catalogue record for this book is available from the British Library.

ISBN 978 1 84797 426 6

WEST SUSSEX LIBRARY SERVICE	
201251014	
Askews & Holts	10-Sep-2013
629.13252	

Typeset by SR Nova Pvt Ltd., Bangalore, India

Printed and bound in India by Replika Press Pvt Ltd

Contents

Dedication	4
Acknowledgements	5
Introduction	6
1 Before You Start Your CPL	13
2 Pre-Course Requirements	20
3 Pre-Lesson and Pre-Flight Checks	23
4 Circuits	34
5 General Airwork	43
6 Instrument Flying	51
7 Navigation	64
8 Emergencies	77
9 170A and CPL Skill Test	86
10 Common Student Mistakes and Failure Points	96
11 After the CPL...	101
12 Privileges of a CPL	103
Useful Information	106
Glossary of Terms & Abbreviations	108
Index	112

Dedication

This book is dedicated to all my students – past, present and future. I am truly blessed to be able to call myself CPL and PPL instructor.

Acknowledgements

Flying is more than a sport and more than a job; flying is pure passion and desire, which fill a lifetime.
A. Galland

To mention all those that have a place in my heart (and log book) would take forever, but those who deserve a special mention are my parents, Jane and Don, for their continued love, moral and financial support.

I would like to thank all those that gave their time and help in the preparation of this book, including all those at Crowood. I am truly grateful to Jane for proof-reading all my efforts, who now knows more about commercial flying than she ever should have, without having a PPL or CPL! I must thank Steve for his humour, diligence and support during the last few stages of the publishing process as well as Chris, Tony and Rob for their very useful feedback. And thanks to John and Steve for being 'model' CPL students.

I would also like to thank all those who have helped me during my long and eventful flying career – from my first trial lesson on my sixteenth birthday (an unexpected but truly amazing gift), through the PPL, the CPL, the ATPLs, the FI course, the IR and the CPL instructional course. So Nick, Andy, Pete, Lee, Tony, Brian and Annabel – thank you. And all those instructors past and present at Stapleford Flight Centre – they are a pleasure to work with and share the skies of England with.

My soul is in the sky.
William Shakespeare – A Midsummer Night's Dream,
Act V, Scene 1

INTRODUCTION

To most people, the sky is the limit. To those who love aviation, the sky is home.

Anon.

Welcome to *The Commercial Pilot's Licence*, or, everything you wanted to know about the CPL but were afraid to ask!

As a private and commercial instructor with over 3,500 hours instructing experience, I have had the pleasure and privilege of seeing hundreds of students start training for their CPL as well as their PPL with the dream of becoming a commercial pilot. But most of them did not seem to know, realistically, what was involved; they had many expectations and assumptions about the kind of flying that was required, but they had no real understanding of what was involved or the skills required to fulfil their dream – not that much different from me when I decided to be a commercial pilot.

When I first wanted to be a commercial pilot, I wanted the thrill of teaching people to fly. But I had absolutely no idea about what I would have to do, as far as flying training was concerned, to get this licence. Some of the questions I remember asking my CPL instructor were: do I have to fly any instrument procedures or approaches? Do we get to go into controlled airspace and fly in the airways with the big shiny jets? Is this it?

So, what is the CPL course really all about? This book aims to dispel some common misconceptions and to help you to get a commercial pilot licence with a first-time pass and so becoming a better pilot. It will hopefully tell you in an easy and user-friendly way what you need to know and how to achieve a first-time pass. It is broken down into three parts. Chapters 1 and 2 look at things to consider before you start the CPL; Chapters 3 to 8 cover the CPL syllabus sections; and Chapters 9 to 13 look at what happens during the test and after. The book breaks the exercises you will fly with your instructor into easy, bite-sized chunks to get you ready for that all-important skill test. It aims to make the course more transparent and to make what is expected of you in each lesson more obvious; the book also contains hints and tips I have picked up over the years of instructing and talking to examiners to hopefully get you that first-time pass. (Whatever you may think or hear, the majority of airlines *are* interested in how many attempts it took you to pass your CPL and Instrument Ratings, and it is often asked on application forms. A series one pass is better than a series two pass.)

So why do you want or even need this book? There are other books available in specialist aviation shops and online that advise you on how to become a private pilot, or how to be a better or safer pilot, or how to become a commercial pilot, and describe the routes taken by the respective authors, but that is not what this book seeks to do. It is your guide to getting through the CPL course and is intended to sit beside the training notes from your training organization to give you the best head start in your professional training.

As you may or may not already know, there is no standard route to becoming a commercial pilot. Every commercial pilot you speak to will have a different story of how and where they did their training, how long it took and what they had to do to get there. The only common thread in the stories of their training is that they will have (at some stage) got the following:

- PPL
- night qualification
- a certain amount of hours as PIC (pilot-in-command)
- CPL

In the case of those who have gone on to get an Air Transport Pilot's Licence (ATPL), the list will go on to include the following:

- Multi-Engine Rating (MEP)
- Instrument Rating (IR)
- Multi Crew Co-Operation Course (MCC)
- Jet Orientation Course (JOC)
- Type Rating on a specific aircraft

Introduction

The main purpose of this book is to help you get the most out of your CPL course as you go through it. But then why not just use the course notes you will have been given by your Aviation Training Organization (ATO)*? Often such course notes tell you *what* you will have to fly but not *how* to fly it. This book offers real practical advice on the lesson content and how to fly the manoeuvres, rather than just a list of what you are expected to know at the end of it. Although there is nothing in the course that is particularly difficult to fly (that fact alone can cause some disappointment), the standard and quality of flying required right from the beginning can be a real shock to some students – I know that I would have really benefited (especially financially) from a book like this before I started my professional training.

Having touched on the subject of financing and cost, here is some advice on financing the CPL. Everyone in the aviation industry knows how expensive flight training is, especially if you want to go all the way and become an airline pilot, and there are precious few ways and means of becoming a commercial pilot that aren't self-funded. However, there are some bursaries and scholarships available for students from various organizations and charities. Details of them can be found in flying magazines and newspapers (such as *Flight Training News*), especially at the beginning of a new year. Obviously, there will be restrictions on age or experience, or what kind of training you are doing, but do some research and apply for them if you fulfil the required conditions, as the money has to go to someone. I was lucky enough to receive a bursary from the Air League when I was training, which helped me enormously in the early years, so a big thank you goes to them!

This book is organized into chapters that follow the various sections of the syllabus to make the best use of your (and your instructor's) time in the air and on the ground. It is meant to be

---

* Flying Training Organizations (FTOs), as they have long been known, were renamed Aviation Training Organizations (ATOs) when new EASA rules and regulations came into force in April 2012.

used in conjunction with whatever course notes you have been given by your training organization, though if in doubt you should always defer to your instructor. However, the ultimate goal is for you to minimize the hours it takes to complete the course: that is to say, ideally, for you not to exceed the minimum number of hours required (25). By reading and implementing what you have read here, hopefully you won't make the mistakes that so many others have. Learn from the mistakes of those who have gone before you, rather than making the same mistakes yourself: it is quicker and also cheaper that way.

Everything written here is intended to help you to become the best possible professional pilot, with a sensible and mature attitude. But that doesn't mean you can't have a sense of humour! You will no doubt have read other books on flying and maybe some training notes, and some of them can be a little dry to read, so I have deliberately tried to make this as easy going as I can. The best CPL students I have flown with and trained are the ones that have learned the drills, and can follow the procedures, be ahead of the aircraft and still be able to crack a smile ... but then switch immediately back into professional pilot mode when required. Flying is meant to be fun, as well as a career. Study hard, do your homework, and learn the drills and procedures, but retain your sense of humour and you will be a real asset to a company as well as a pleasure to fly with.

An important point that often comes up on the course – usually as we get near the end – is that students have been told at the beginning of the course, or when they sign up, that the CPL course is 25 hours long (if you don't already have a CPL or IR). There follows, therefore, an inherent assumption that it will only take you 25 hours' flying time before you hold that pass certificate in your hand. However, it often doesn't work out like that in real life. It is quite likely that you will not be ready for test in 25 hours; in fact, not many people are ready to test at 25 hours at all. The average is 28–33 hours, not including the test itself, which takes about 2 hours.

Hopefully, using this book will help you reduce the hours you will need to get to test standard, but everyone is different and there can be many reasons why you may need more than

Introduction

25 hours: lack of continuity because of bad weather, lack of familiarity with the UK's airspace, sickness, aeroplanes going unserviceable, personal and financial problems, or simply because you haven't done enough homework and 'arm-chair flying'.

You would do well to budget for at least 28–30 hours of flying training (not including the flight test itself) to be on the safe side. Nothing is more stressful for a student than being ready for the skill test, but then working out or being told by your ATO that you are running out of money so you can't finish the extra hours or pay for the test. You should also make sure you have enough when you start the course as no sensible school will allow you to start flying training without the necessary funds available. Make sure you agree with the ATO ahead of time how you will be paying and have the funds available on your first day. This often catches out students from overseas who rely on bank transfers or loans. Remember to factor in that it takes time for money to be transferred from overseas as no money in your bank account = no flying.

If you do the entire CPL course on the complex aircraft type (that is, with retractable undercarriage and a constant-speed propeller) that you will eventually do the CPL test in, you will probably complete the course and be ready for the skill test in fewer total hours than if you start in a basic aircraft and then move on to the complex type later on. Obviously the exact saving will depend on the school and your own personal circumstances, so you should work it out for yourself before you start. It may make the early part of the course a little more expensive but it will potentially be cheaper in the long run to do 25 hours in a complex type rather than 30 hours in a mixture of two aircraft types. Also, as you will be more familiar with the aircraft, you are more likely to help yourself to that first-time pass.

If you are feeling a little nervous about starting the CPL and worrying that you may not be able to fly as well expected, don't forget that your instructor went through much the same challenges in their own training as you may well do. (I know that I made every mistake in the book!) Keep in mind that your instructor is there to guide you to passing the course, and that they will always do what they can to help you improve, and help to get the best out of you and your time in the air. So listen to them and take their advice – good or bad. It is likely that your instructor will have seen pretty much all of the mistakes that can and do occur during CPL training and will be well versed in spotting them. The CPL course may come across in the first few lessons as being a rather expensive way to be told that everything you learnt as a PPL is not good enough, but it is always constructive criticism designed to make you into a great professional pilot, and your instructor has only your best interest at heart. So: listen to them, make notes in the pre- and post-flight briefings, ask questions (whether you think they are silly or not), sit in the back seat of other student training flights and mentally critique what they are doing wrong, take the course seriously and you will not go far wrong.

This book is a practical flying guide to the CPL course only: it is not trying to be a book on how to get a commercial flying job. If you want advice on how to get an airline job, the best person to ask is a current airline pilot. I have deliberately not gone into the Multi-Pilot Licence or Instrument Rating as that would fill another book for another time. And also note that this book is based upon conducting the CPL course on a single-engine, complex aeroplane such as the Piper Arrow, so if you are planning to do the course on a different aircraft, then you will need to refer to your instructor and/or POH for the important aspects such as speeds. Also, it follows a modular CPL training syllabus in the UK. If you intend on following the integrated course route, the way you get to the CPL may be different but the skill test is still pretty much the same, and there will still be useful information in here for you.

For those of you who aren't sure of the difference between integrated and modular CPL courses: an integrated course means you stay with the same training organization from the PPL, through the hour building, the night rating and CPL, then onto the Multi Rating and Instrument Rating and possibly through to the Multi-Crew course and Jet Orientation Course and type rating needed to fly the big jets. These tend to be done over a shorter time as it is full-time study and flying, and tends to be more expensive than the modular route. The modular route involves doing exactly the same training but with different training organizations, possibly over a few years. It tends to attract

Introduction

students that have decided to become a commercial pilot later in life or have family commitments, or don't have the money upfront to pay for the flying training all in one go, which can be in excess of £90,000 from the day of your first lesson to getting a type rating and being ready to fly as an airline pilot.

And one final bit of advice that will serve you well if you keep it in mind:

> *Never let an aircraft take you somewhere your brain didn't get to 5 minutes earlier.*
>
> *Anon.*

1 Before You Start Your CPL

Once you have tasted flight, you will forever walk the earth with your eyes turned skyward, for there you have been, and there you will always long to return.
                                                            Leonardo da Vinci

If you are still reading this, then congratulations: you are one step nearer to gaining your CPL. You have probably already come through quite a journey of a PPL, hours building and those infamously tough CPL or Airline Transport Pilot's Licence (ATPL) exams, and so hopefully you are ready to start your commercial training.

If, however, you have just finished your PPL, or you haven't yet finished your hour building, or not yet selected an ATO for your training, this chapter contains some advice before we get to the really fun bits of the actual flying.

Firstly, let's talk about hour building. If you have not yet got the 100 hours as Pilot in Command (PIC) that you need to be issued with a CPL, or the 150 total hours needed to start the course, you should think about the hour building you need to do and come up with a sensible plan for it. If you just muck about with no structure or spend it mostly in the circuit or your local area, you could find that you will be using the first few hours of your CPL course re-learning the basics, forcing the instructor to get rid of the bad flying habits you have allowed to develop. This will cost you dearly in time and money, and will certainly mean more hours needed to finish the course. For example, I spend a lot of time re-teaching students how to trim and reminding them to look out of the window, scanning the sky for traffic from wing tip to wing tip – because there was no one sitting next to you nagging you to do it properly while you are hours building alone – as well as brushing students up on their sloppy RT calls.

There are various ways to hour build, but ideally the end result should be that it enhances your flying ability, command experience and general competence – as well as being fun. A major decision can be whether to do your hour building in the UK or abroad.

The pros and cons of hour building outside the UK are as follows:

- ✓ Possibly all round good weather
- ✓ The experience of flying abroad
- ✓ Usually cheaper than the UK
- ✗ Not being able to see the school before you sign up or the aircraft or the facilities before you go
- ✗ Being away from home
- ✗ Lack of familiarity with UK airspace, RT procedures and so on when you return
- ✗ Maybe having to fly a few extra hours to get you up to speed on UK procedures

The pros and cons of hour building in the UK are as follows:

- ✓ Getting a good grounding in UK airspace and RT procedures
- ✓ Access to the schools to visit for advice
- ✓ Excellent standard of training
- ✓ Easy access to instructors for advice and guidance
- ✗ Potentially inconsistent weather
- ✗ Generally more expensive unless you buy hours in bulk

If you decide to go abroad for your hour building, it can't be emphasized enough that you could save a lot of time and money on the CPL course if you 'save' about 5 hours of your hour building for the UK and, more specifically, the airfield where you will do your CPL training. Get hold of a CPL instructor (not literally!), offer to buy them a hearty breakfast and pick their brains on how and what they teach in the course, what advice they can give you and what they are looking for.

Get useful information from them such as navigation routes, airfields, school-specific aircraft internal and external checks,

> **Top Tip**
>
> Try to find some friends or fellow PPLs to go with you when hour building. It will be so much more enjoyable as very few people enjoy flying on their own, and you can share the costs of accommodation, food and landing fees. It is a bizarre fact, but you will often find that friends and indeed comparative strangers are more likely to want to come flying with you rather than your family, so don't be too disappointed if your relatives won't come with you.

the course notes and so on, so you can start to incorporate it into your last few hours of solo flying. I would even go as far as recommending that you get yourself booked in for a lesson with a CPL instructor prior to the start of your CPL course, so you can ask for their honest feedback as to the quality of your flying and what you could do to improve. It may be an additional expense but it is well worth it.

If you haven't yet selected an ATO for your CPL, you should give a lot of thought to the following points. You must identify all of your own and the training school's requirements, your own current qualifications and experience, and so on, before making any decision about any signing up and parting with your money:

- How much does the course cost, and does the price include approach fees, test fees, landing fees, any fuel surcharges, and ground school?
- What time of the year do you plan to start your training? Training in the summer is going to be better from a continuity point of view, as you won't be interrupted by bad weather.
- What type of aircraft will you fly. Will you stay on a complex type for the whole course, or will you start on a basic aircraft first and then move on to the complex type?
- Will you work full-time and fly part-time, or will you train full time? Don't underestimate how tiring the training will

be and how much studying you will have to do. Flying part-time at weekends will always increase the amount of time and money spent getting to test standard compared with training on a full-time basis.
- Are you required to pay up-front or pay as you go? Will you get a discount if you pay up front?
- Are there any financial issues or other problems at home that may cause you to be distracted and unable to concentrate fully?
- Will you stay on site or will you have to commute a long distance to get to the school?
- Lastly, are there any medical or licence issues that need to be resolved with the Civil Aviation Authority (CAA) before you start the course?

A good place to start your search for an ATO is the CAA website, www.caa.co.uk. It lists all the schools in the UK and abroad approved by the CAA to conduct the CPL course. The CPL is one of the most valued of all licences and should be what you are aiming to hold. If you don't get an EASA FCL licence to start with – that is, if you go to a non-EASA country to do your training – you may well have to convert it when you start job hunting. The re-training to upgrade to an EASA licence is 'as required' as there are no specific or minimum hours required.

It makes sense to compare the course requirements and other details of the schools you are interested in, and to visit them – some will have open days that will formally introduce you to the school, the facilities and the instructors. Also try to arrange a visit on a normal working day so you can get the feel of the place. Don't be afraid to talk to students who are training there and instructors that work there, as most of them will be more than happy to give you advice and share their experiences.

In addition to the specific items listed above, issues to think about are: aircraft and instructor availability; pass rates; number of aircraft available; accommodation availability; any additional or hidden costs; and on-site aircraft maintenance – a school that has its own maintenance facility on-site is a useful commodity. Also ask about links to airlines and the number of CPL/IR students that get airline jobs. Don't be afraid to ask whether you will have to 'pay as you go', in instalments or even the whole amount up front. Ask about any discounts for payments up front. Do bear in mind, though, that ATOs can and do go bankrupt, so be sensible about any 'too good to be true' deals.

Try to avoid believing everything you read on pilot internet forums. The comments posted range from the really useful to the not so useful, and then to the downright biased; the latter usually from individuals who have a grudge against certain parts of the aviation world. However, don't disregard them completely and if you read something you aren't sure about, ask another pilot. An interesting question to ask an ATO is how they feel about and react to any negative feedback. But the best way to get a balanced view is to talk to as many people as possible about how and where they did their training: what did they enjoy and what do they wish they had done differently?

You must keep in mind that most people will go over the 25 hours to complete the course, so you should realistically budget for at least an extra 3 hours as well as extra for the approach/landing fees. You will also need to budget for any in-school 170A test fees, changes in VAT and/or fuel surcharges. Lastly, the cost of the CPL skill test is, in early 2012, £780 (and that amount will only ever go up), not including the hire of the aircraft and landing fees. Add all these up and you don't want to find yourself in the situation where you are ready for the test and don't have the money to do it.

It may seem a strange thing to put in this book, but do not get too excited or get your hopes up about the CPL course being the easiest or best flying of your life (so far). It may seem as if you have already spent a long time and a lot of money getting this far, and you have probably made some huge personal sacrifices along the way to start the CPL course itself, and looking forward to it is what got you through the ATPL exams ... but believe it or not, the course can be a disappointment for some. There is a huge but also a subtle difference in what is expected from you as a professional pilot compared with the flying you did with your PPL instructor and with your friends while hour building on a sunny day. Some have called the CPL a glorified PPL and I can see their point, but what we are doing is laying the groundwork that will take you through the rest of your professional training.

Having said all that, it must be emphasized that pretty much everyone who starts a CPL course will finish it. Whether it takes 25 hours or 50, you will get through it and in minimum time if you do as you are told, read this book and study hard. Most cases of people failing to finish are to do with financial or personal problems, so try your best to eliminate as many of those as possible before you start for the best possible results.

I always tell my students right from the very first lesson that CPL instructors are paid to teach as well as nag – because commercial flying is always about professionalism, good planning, safety consciousness, having a high degree of situational awareness, good passenger care and excellent aircraft handling ability, and I train my students until those standards of flying are second nature. Some of my students may not have always agreed with me, and they may not even have liked what I have had to say, but it is only said and done to get you a first-time pass. If you find yourself wanting something else to look forward to, the multi-rating is great fun!

Here are some questions I have been asked over the years that may be of some help to you:

Should I choose modular or integrated training?
While integrated is more expensive, it is full time and totally focussed on getting you ready for the airlines in the shortest amount of time. This suits some and not others, as it is very intense. There is also no guarantee of a job with an airline at the end, despite what some organizations say, but they do have very close links with certain airlines who may look on your application favourably. However, modular or part-time training can be more flexible and is better for those who are training in between work and family commitments, those that have to train in different countries and schools, and those who can't afford the integrated schools' charges. If you are reading this book, then modular is probably the way forward for you.

Should I do the CPL or the IR first?
It has been my experience that for 99.9 per cent of students, the CPL should definitely be done first. It gives you the professional standard of flying required in a Visual Flight Rules

(VFR) environment before doing all that and much more under Instrument Flight Rules (IFR). Unless you are unusual in that you have a lot of instrument flying (IF) time, I strongly recommend you do the CPL first.

Should I do all my CPL training on a complex aircraft type?
If you have the option, I would recommend you do all the CPL course on a complex type as this is the aircraft you will be tested in and will be more comfortable in. Some schools offer the first 15 hours in a basic aircraft to make the initial cost of the course cheaper, but that only leaves 5 hours in the complex type (as the other 5 can be in the simulator), which often isn't enough time for the student to feel totally confident in it. I have found that students are most likely to pass the first time in minimum hours if they train on the complex type from the beginning.

Should I practise some or all exercises of the CPL course on a computer at home or a simulator?
In a word, no! Please don't. If you must, then only practise the instrument flying: if you practise the rest of the syllabus (which is meant to be under VFR) on a computer, then you will probably fly very nicely on instruments, but you risk failing to develop a good lookout technique, which can be a fail point in the skill test, and not using good visual flying techniques, i.e. not using the visual horizon in all of your manoeuvres.

As a final point in this chapter, do read the most common mistakes and fail points at the end of this book. You will save yourself a lot of time and money, both in the air and on the ground if you read them and try to avoid making them yourself.

2 Pre-Course Requirements

We who fly do so for the love of flying. We are alive in the air with this miracle that lies in our hands and beneath our feet.

Cecil Lewis

If you turn up on your first day (on a modular course) with the wrong documents or licence requirements (or no money), then you can't start the CPL course, no matter how much you beg or plead: you must be sure you have everything you need. I will explain the requirements below, but the same information can now be found in CAP 804. (The requirements used to be found in the CAA publication *LASORS*.) EASA rules and regulations came into force during 2012 and the syllabus remained unchanged, but students are always well advised to keep up to date with future changes to the licence and training, and these can be found on the CAA website.

BEFORE YOU START

Before you start the modular course, you need the following:

- A valid SEP PPL (A).
- At least 150 hours total time in your log book.
- A valid form of ID i.e. a passport or driving licence, and any necessary visas that allow you to train in the UK if you are not a UK resident. Contact the CAA if you are at all unsure if you need a visa.
- You must be over 18 years old.
- If you don't hold a night qualification before you start the course, you may start the CPL training and do the night qualification alongside it, but the hours flown at night cannot be included as part of the 25 hours for the CPL.

Pre-Course Requirements

- You must have passed all the CPL(Aeroplane) or ATPL (Aeroplane) written exams – nine exams for a CPL or fourteen for the ATPL. Do note that if you opt to take only the nine CPL exams but then decide to apply for an ATPL, you will have to sit the full fourteen ATPL exams, as the nine you already passed are not included!
- You must have held a Class 1 medical at some point in time; if you have had a initial Class 1 but it has not been renewed, the Class 1 can have lapsed to a Class 2.

THE CPL COURSE

The course itself is a minimum of 25 hours of dual flight (so all the training flights are logged as P.U.T). Ten of these hours (minimum) must be instrument flying, of which 5 can be in an approved simulator.

The skill test must be taken on a complex type aircraft, i.e. retractable undercarriage and variable-pitch propeller and can be on a single-engine or multi-engine aircraft.

TO APPLY FOR THE CPL LICENCE

Once you have passed the CPL skill test, you will need to apply for the licence itself. Before you can do this, you must have:

- 200 hours in your log book (total time) of which 100 hours must be pilot in command.
- 20 hours of VFR cross-country flight time as pilot in command, including one flight that is at least 300nm long with two full-stop landings at two aerodromes not including the aerodromes you took off from or landed at. This can done during the CPL course itself but is not included in the 25-hour course minimum.
- 10 hours of dual instrument flying in your logbook, 5 of which can be in an approved simulator.
- A night qualification.
- 100 hours pilot in command in your logbook.
- A valid radio licence and English Proficiency Certificate. Contact the CAA if you are unsure if you need the English Proficiency Certificate.

Pre-Course Requirements

OTHER IMPORTANT INFORMATION

The CPL or ATPL written exams are valid for 36 months from the date of the pass in your last written exam. If you don't complete and pass the CPL and IR skill tests and get the licence issued within the 36 month period, the exams become invalid and have to be sat again. So be careful: I know at least two students that didn't get their training done in time and so had to re-sit all fourteen ATPL exams.

> ### Top Tip
>
> If you haven't done so already, get your initial Class 1 medical booked at Gatwick (if you are UK-based) and passed before you apply for or start your course. You should have been told that you have to have a Class 1 medical for a CPL before committing yourself to the ATPL or CPL exams, but if you haven't, you will want to find out about any medical issues before you commit time and money to the course. The most common problems with the medical are related to colour blindness and heart problems.

If you are unsure of what is required or you have a foreign PPL, medical or RT licence then you should read the appropriate section in CAP 804. However if you are unsure or can't find the answer to a complicated licence issue, contact your training school or look at the CAA website, or even contact the CAA at Gatwick directly. You really don't want to do all the training and spend all that money, and then find out it was all for nothing.

Lastly, there are no land-aways, no airways work, no (intentional) trips into controlled airspace or instrument procedures. You will have plenty of time to master these in the IR.

3 Pre-Lesson and Pre-Flight Checks

Things which do you no good in aviation: altitude above you; fuel in the truck; runway behind you; approach plates in the car and the airspeed you don't have.

Anon.

BEFORE THE LESSON

To get the most out of your training, you need to arrive at least 30 minutes before the start of each lesson. This is so that you can get the aircraft checked and ready, re-fuel and top up the oil if required, complete the tech log, review the current NOTAMS

A Piper Arrow on the stand.

Pre-Lesson and Pre-Flight Checks

> **Top Tip**
>
> Get used to filling in the tech log for each flight, having noted the following:
>
> - The correct date
> - Airframe hours are within date
> - Date of the next maintenance check
> - Validity period of the ARC (Airworthiness Review Certificate)
>
> Also, note any 'snags' that may have arisen from the previous flight, and check that the Certificate of Release to Service matches the tech log, i.e. the dates due and the airframe hours match each other exactly. If they don't, or you have any questions, ask your instructor or at reception.

for the flight profile (www.ais.org.uk), check the weather (www.metoffice.gov.uk/aviation) and prepare any lesson plan.

Be pro-active: don't rely on your instructor to have done these preliminaries, or wait for them to get back from their previous lesson. (They try their best, but on busy flying days, instructors can and do run a little late.) This kind of approach will start to give you responsibility for organizing yourself, your paperwork and your flights, now and in the future. If you can be ready to fly at the start of the lesson time (rather than be finishing a cup of tea and thinking about heading out to the aircraft), you will get the most out of it.

Make sure you get the flight authorized by the instructor – usually done by them initialling the tech log. You, however, can fill in the expected fuel and oil at the start of the flight, the departure and arrival aerodrome and lesson type, as well as initialling the Check A. (Each school will have slightly different formats for their tech logs, but initialling the Check A means that you have conducted a thorough walk-around of the aircraft

Pre-Lesson and Pre-Flight Checks

> **Top Tip**
>
> At the end of each lesson, make a note of your flight times, the exercise number and the number of take-offs and landings, as this will mean that your log book will match the tech log and your student record. This will hopefully reduce the time spent checking that they all match up as you approach your test, as the instructor needs to make sure that you have completed every exercise and reached the appropriate hours for test.

and that it is fit to fly.) Your instructor will make a note of the times of the flight, as different schools have different ways of logging the length of the flight.

You should already be reasonably competent at completing the tech log, because wherever you did your training and hours building, you should have been filling them in. If, however, you are at all unsure, then ask your instructor for advice.

The aircraft you are due to use may well be flying in the time slot before your lesson, so if there is a chance of running late, you might suggest taking another aircraft instead so that you get the most of your lesson time. Even a 2-hour slot can be reduced to only 45 minutes in the air if none of the preparation listed above has been done. The aircraft checks (internal and external) for the CPL are more time-consuming than the PPL. It can take up to 30 minutes from door closed to ready for departure if you are unfamiliar with the checklist.

It may sound obvious, but as you walk out to the aircraft, check its position relative to other aircraft, the taxy way and any possible obstructions. Many students climb in and start the pre-flight checks oblivious of the fact that they need to push back away from the nearest aircraft to avoid hitting it. Telling the examiner that the obstruction should not have been on the taxy way is not a good reason to hit it as you go past. (I am afraid that this is actually what happened on one particular skill test!)

Pre-Lesson and Pre-Flight Checks

PRE-FLIGHT CHECKS

There should be two checklists in the aircraft: this is a requirement for the aircraft used and authorized for CPL training. Use one of them for the walk-around and the internal checks, as they have been approved by the CAA. You will want to be at the stage where the instructor can join you once all these checks have been completed and you are ready to start the internal checks under the instructor's supervision.

Make sure the instrument screens or hood (if that is what you use) are on the back seat, in the right order and within reach in case a lesson plan has to change or you have to do some instrument flying.

If there is a problem with the aircraft, check with your instructor or another instructor, or with an engineer if available. If it is an equipment issue – such as an instrument failure on the internal check – check the MEL (Minimum Equipment List) to see if the aircraft can nonetheless be used for the planned lesson. A copy of the MEL should be kept in the tech log and with the aircraft documents, as well as the POH.

Use the checklist slowly and carefully, and as a challenge and response: read out the item on the list and the action you are doing. Keep a careful note of how far you have gone down the checklist and, if you lose your place, go back to the start and do them again so that you don't miss any of the checks out. It is frighteningly easy to miss something, especially the supposedly really obvious things.

Here is the patter you will need to learn for the internal instrument checks. Obviously, if any of these checks are wrong, the flight needs to be abandoned. If you refer to the picture of the Piper Arrow cockpit you will see that we are going to start at the top left-hand corner and then go across the cockpit from left to right, checking every instrument. Obviously every aircraft is different, so you will need to alter your own instrument checks from this order to reflect the instrument panel of your aircraft.

Compass: Place your hand under the compass and say it is 'secure'. Say 'No leaks, no discoloration of the fluid, no bubbles, the deviation card is in date (three years from the date shown on the card) and is reading a sensible heading.'

Pre-Lesson and Pre-Flight Checks

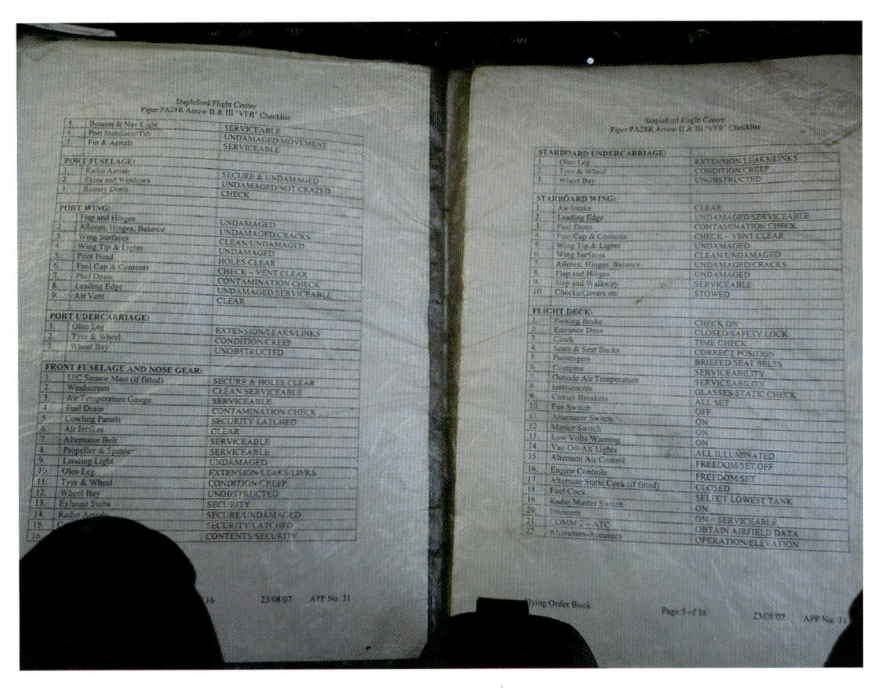

CPL checklist.

Instrument screens.

27

Pre-Lesson and Pre-Flight Checks

Cockpit of the Piper Arrow.

OAT: Place your hand under the temperature gauge, try to move it and say it is 'secure' (if it is). Say 'The OAT is consistent with the day's forecast.'

Now work your way across the cockpit, going through each instrument in turn, wherever they are positioned:

Clock: Make sure it is reading the correct time. This must be Zulu/GMT, not local time.

ASI: Say 'No cracks, reading zero and will check it after start.'

AI: Say 'no cracks' and, it being a gyro instrument, 'I will check it after start.'

Altimeter 1: Say 'No cracks. Set apron elevation.' Move the winder through zero to the left and to the right and say 'increasing increasing' then 'decreasing decreasing'. What this means is that as you wind the pointer back through zero, the altimeter indication should reduce as should the millibars (hectopascals) and/or inches of mercury as displayed, and then the opposite should happen when you move the pointer through zero and increasing. Set the apron elevation, which should be similar to the QNH given by ATC when you call up.

Suction: Say 'No cracks and I will check it after start.'

Ammeter: Say 'No cracks and I will check it after start.'

ADF: Say 'No cracks and I will check it after start.'

Turn co-ordinator: Say 'No cracks and I will check it after start.' Also say 'The failure flag should be showing.'

DI: Say 'No cracks and I will check it after start.' If it is an HSI, then you also need to say 'Nav 1 is needle centred, failure flag showing and I will check it after start.'

VSI: Say 'No cracks and I will check it after start.' It should be within limits of plus or minus 200 feet.

Engine instruments: Say 'Manifold pressure reading ambient [if it is] and I will check the rest after start.'

GPS/comms units: Say 'I will check after start.'

> ## Top Tip
> - Sit in the aircraft when you don't have a lesson or it is a bad weather day, and practise the internal checks and instrument checks; this will save you time and money each lesson. The quicker you can become familiar with these checks, the quicker you will get into the air.
> - To avoid embarrassing mistakes, before you press the Press To Transmit (PTT) button, you must check three things: that you have the correct frequency, that you have the correct comms unit in use, and that the volume is suitable (check this last by operating the squelch). Doing this every single time (*before* you transmit) means that you won't transmit on the wrong frequency or step on anyone else's transmission because the volume is turned down.
> - Don't call the comms units 'boxes'.

PASSENGER BRIEFING

You will be expected to give a passenger brief at some point, usually before engine start. Your ATO will probably provide you with one of these, but in case they don't I have provided an example of what should be said. Note that is it specific to the Piper Arrow, so amend it as required for your aircraft type.

> Ladies and Gentleman, welcome on board your flight in this Piper Arrow. There is a seatbelt of either a lap belt and shoulder harness or just a lap belt on either side of your seat. I will be happy to demonstrate how to operate it if you are unfamiliar with its design. Please ensure you are familiar with its operation before take-off. There is an exit door to your right. The door is opened by moving the top latch forward and the bottom lever upwards and pushing the door outwards.
>
> This is a non-smoking flight so please do not smoke inside or outside the aircraft. I would also ask you to please turn off all mobile phones and electrical devices until we are at our destination. If you are sitting alongside the pilot in the front, please do not touch any of the aircraft controls; if you inadvertently touch something, please do not hesitate to tell me.
>
> In the event of an emergency, I will ask you to remain calm. If I call out BRACE, BRACE, BRACE, I would ask you to assume the BRACE position like this [demonstrate] with your hands on your head, the elbows tucked in and your head lowered. If we are required to make an emergency landing, please take up the BRACE position. Be sure to remove any glasses, false teeth and any sharp objects as well as making sure your harness is tight and the seat back is upright before landing. Once the aircraft has come to a complete stop, remove your harness and exit the aircraft to the rear. Should we need it, there is a First Aid Kit in the seat back [demonstrate] and a fire extinguisher between the seats [demonstrate]. A copy of this brief can be found in the rear seat back, which I recommend that you read.

TAXYING

Once all the pre-start, after-start and comms checks have been completed as per the checklist, you must do a brake check as soon as you start to taxy. Do not wait to get onto the tarmac and do not ride the brakes once you are underway – we know when you are doing it because we can hear the engine racing. To do the brake test, apply enough power to get the wheels rolling, then close the throttle, apply the brakes firmly and bring the aircraft to a stop. Then ask your instructor or examiner if they

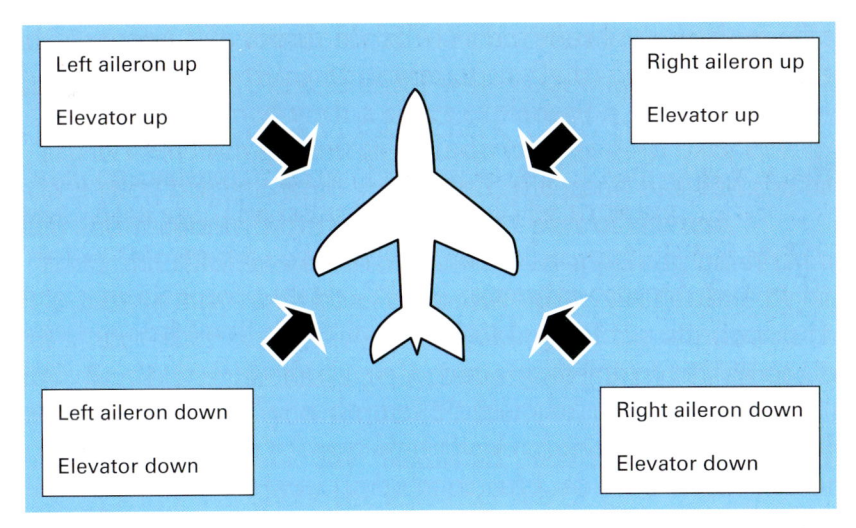

| Left aileron up | Right aileron up |
| Elevator up | Elevator up |

| Left aileron down | Right aileron down |
| Elevator down | Elevator down |

Where you should be putting the ailerons while taxing in various wind directions.

would like to check their brakes. They should check their brakes and then give control back to you. Don't forget to say 'I have control and 'You have control.' And always position the ailerons appropriately in relation to the wind when taxying.

Be aware of other aircraft movements, especially if it is an uncontrolled and/or busy training airfield. Take the most direct way to the area for your run-up checks and to the correct area for the runway in use. Try to anticipate obstructions: soggy, rutted or boggy ground, and other student pilots who will need a wide berth. Taxy speeds tend to increase as confidence and hours grow, so remember to keep to a slow walking speed only.

You will need to find some room on the way to the hold to do the taxy checks, ideally before you get there. You should try to do four small turns: two to the left and two to the right. As you turn left, say 'Decreasing, decreasing, tracking.' What you are checking is that as you turn left, the compass and DI/HSI turn and the headings decrease, and the ADF/RMI needle is moving; then, rather obviously, in the right turn, you are checking is that as you turn right, the compass and DI/HSI turn and the headings increase and the ADF/RMI needle is moving.

Then repeat the turn left, and say 'Turn left, ball right, AI steady.' What you are checking is that as you turn left, the turn co-ordinator turns left, the balance ball slips right and the AI

Pre-Lesson and Pre-Flight Checks

Turn 4: Compass numbers decreasing, DI numbers decreasing, ADF needle tracking

Turn 3: Compass numbers increasing, DI numbers increasing, ADF needle tracking

Turn 2: Turn left, ball right on turn co-ordinator, AI steady

Turn 1: Turn right, ball left on turn co-ordinator, AI steady

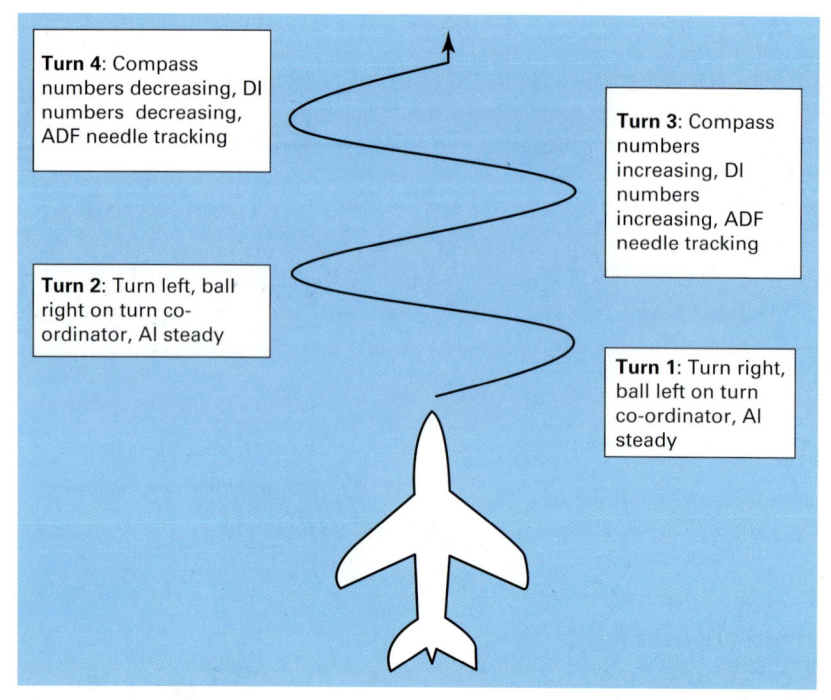

'S' turns for the taxy checks – note that this is not the take-off or landing profile!

remains stable and erect. As you turn right, say 'Turn right, ball left, AI steady.' What you should be checking is that as you turn right, the turn co-ordinator turns right, the balance ball slips left and the AI remains stable and erect.

Once the power checks and pre take-off checks are completed at the designated area using your checklist, taxy to the holding point for the runway in use. You will be expected to give a captain's brief, along with the departure checks before the radio call that you are ready for departure. The power checks and pre-flight checks are aircraft-specific, and should be followed using the checklist that you have been provided with by your instructor. Follow them carefully and thoroughly, and if you think you may have missed a check, go to the top of the checklist and start again. An example of a captain's breif:

> The runway in use is 22L. There is a 5kt wind from the left and it is within the crosswind limits for this aircraft of 17kt. I will

rotate at 70kt clean and accelerate to Vx of 80kt and then above 500ft AGL I will accelerate to Vy of 90kt.

Any aircraft or engine malfunction before 70kt, I will abort the take-off and come to a stop on the remaining runway. If there is a malfunction after rotation, I will lower the nose and land on the remaining runway or in a suitable field, preferably into wind.

Notice that you are effectively briefing yourself on what you will do in the departure and what you will do in the event of an emergency: you are *not* briefing your instructor/the examiner. You should then do the departure checks.

The Departure Checks: FATPL

- Fuel pump on
- Altimeters checked and cross checked with correct QNH
- Transponder set to 7000 and set to Mode C (or appropriate squawk code as given by ATC)
- Pitot heat on
- Landing light on

You also need to check that the DI/HSI and compass are aligned, as these instruments are notorious for wandering off (even if there is a slaving unit), and that the Course Deviation Indicator (CDI) on the HSI is set to the runway orientation so the head of the needle shows the runway in use. This will enable you to immediately see the approximate headings for crosswind, downwind, base leg and final, should you need them when re-joining, and it is something you should set as part of your airfield approach checks.

Lastly, as you line yourself up on the runway don't leave too much runway behind you. Then power up to 2,000rpm while checking that the brakes are holding, that the DI/HSI and compass are aligned, that the temperatures and pressures are in the green and that you are aligned on the correct runway heading. Only if you are satisfied do you apply full power, rudder to keep the aircraft straight, apply crosswind inputs and let her accelerate...

4 Circuits

I give that landing a nine ... on the Richter scale.

Anon.

This is usually the first lesson in the CPL course. It is a chance to familiarize yourself with, quite possibly, a new airfield, new aircraft and new instructor, but doing something that you should be reasonably familiar with – if you go back to your logbook and work out how many hours you have spent in the circuit, you will be very surprised.

However, just because you have done quite a few hours in the circuit doesn't mean that the first circuit lesson of the CPL course always goes smoothly. Don't feel disappointed or annoyed with yourself if you suddenly start flying as if you have never been in an aircraft before, as it happens all the time. The factors listed above seem to all come together into a mixture of poor speed control, poor altitude holding, no pre-landing checks, no fuel tank changes and some pretty dodgy landings. This is all perfectly normal and certainly no indication that you are not capable of being a commercial pilot.

The CPL is all about accuracy, professionalism and safety. Therefore, accurate speed control on the climb-out, base and final is important, as are maintaining altitude on downwind and monitoring the drift in the circuit so that you are always in the correct position on each leg, especially on final approach.

You will be asked to demonstrate a normal approach, a flapless approach, a glide approach and a bad weather circuit. You will also be asked to do a rejected take-off at the end of your skill

> **Top Tip**
>
> With your radio calls, the correct RT call on final is the word 'final'. It is not 'finals' or 'long finals' or 'late finals'. You can only be on final for one runway, which is why it is singular.

test, which will also need to be practised. Make sure you know all the correct (published) speeds, such as the speed over the threshold, as the speeds you give to the examiner will be will be speeds you will be expected to fly. Have a look at Chapter 9 for the tolerance on speeds, as there isn't much of a margin for error.

You could be asked to perform these circuits at your home airfield or at another controlled airfield, or maybe at an international airport on your test, so make sure you know the correct frequencies. Ensure you have an up-to-date photocopy of the plate for the airport you are going to, i.e. a diagram of the runways in use, frequencies in use etc,. that can be downloaded from the AIS website, and do study it so you are familiar with it before you go. Don't forget to call them (if required) to book your circuits as they may not accept a mid-air request.

Some airports charge quite a lot of money for approaches and 'touch and go's, so be prepared for this lesson to keep the approaches down to a minimum: the quicker you get them right, the cheaper it will be. Have the runway in use, and the headings for base and crosswind, in mind using the CDI, and mentally plan the join as soon as you can, especially if you have that information available before you take-off ... but there is no guarantee that they won't change the runway in use before you get there! The join at a controlled airport often becomes a fail point because the student is behind the aircraft and so is slow to make radio calls, late descents, no approach or landing checks and missing traffic in and around the airport.

THE NORMAL CIRCUIT AND APPROACH

This shouldn't be too difficult, but some things to remember are:

- Good positioning in the circuit, taking into account the drift.
- Good spatial awareness of yourself and other aircraft, especially if you are at a busy training airfield. Listening out on the radio is incredibly important.
- Good early decision-making, for example: slowing the aircraft on downwind if you are catching up another slower aircraft ahead (an orbit in the ATZ is not an option), or going around

Circuits

if the approach is unstable or another aircraft has lined up in front of you or cut you up. It all happens and needs to be dealt with promptly and safely.
- Prompt and accurate radio calls. State where you are, which runway and what you are doing: 'G-XXXX final 22L full stop' or 'G-XXXX late downwind 22L touch and go.' Use a 'late' call or 'short' call if required for an accurate picture of your position.
- Accurate altitude and speed control. Remember that the tolerances of speed are +10kt/−5kt and altitude is +100ft/−100ft. The examiner can be lenient with speed and altitude errors up to a degree (especially in turbulent conditions), but it is best to start flying accurately now so that it becomes instinctive for the rest of your professional career.
- Be aware of noise sensitive areas, terrain and all local procedures.

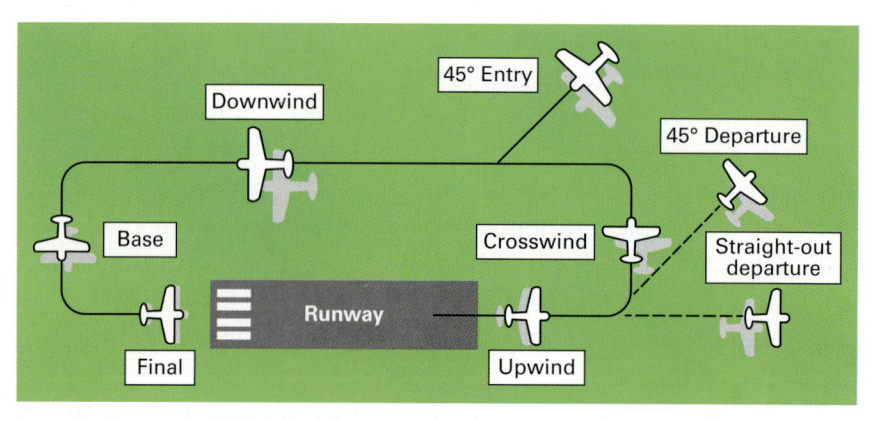

Standard or normal left-hand circuit.

THE FLAPLESS CIRCUIT AND APPROACH

- Remember that you need to extend the downwind leg as well as slowing the aircraft down a little earlier on base (by configuring appropriately) to allow for the lack of drag from the flap.
- Maintain the correct approach speed – it is tempting to lower the nose to see the runway, which results in a speed increase.
- Close the throttle a little earlier approaching or in the flare to allow for the longer float, especially if you are asked to touch down at a certain point.

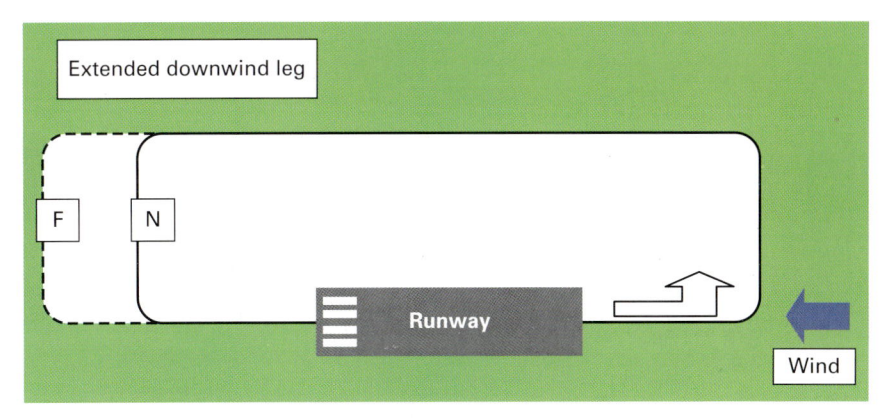

A flapless circuit.

THE GLIDE CIRCUIT AND APPROACH

- Be quick with the downwind calls and pre-landing checks, as it is an early turn onto base.
- Maintain your circuit altitude on base until you are sure you can make the touchdown point with all three stages of flap down. Be aware that on the complex type aircraft, descending in the glide with the landing gear out and flaps down can cause a scarily steep nose-down attitude.
- Only put a stage of flap in once you are you sure you can make it to the touchdown point. Always reset the nose attitude and trim for the best glide speed between each stage of flap.
- Common mistakes are closing the throttle too early on base (the Piper Arrow's glide performance has to be seen to be believed with the gear and three stages of flap on!), not allowing for the strength of the wind, being too high and leaving the decision to go around too late.
- If you are sure you are not going to make the touchdown point, tell the examiner and immediately execute a go-around. Do not transmit that you are going around until you are climbing away and the aircraft is all cleaned up at 90kt. Remember what you were taught on the PPL course – aviate, navigate, then communicate.
- Keep a very good lookout for other circuit traffic, as you are in a non-standard circuit. Give way or go around if necessary.

Circuits

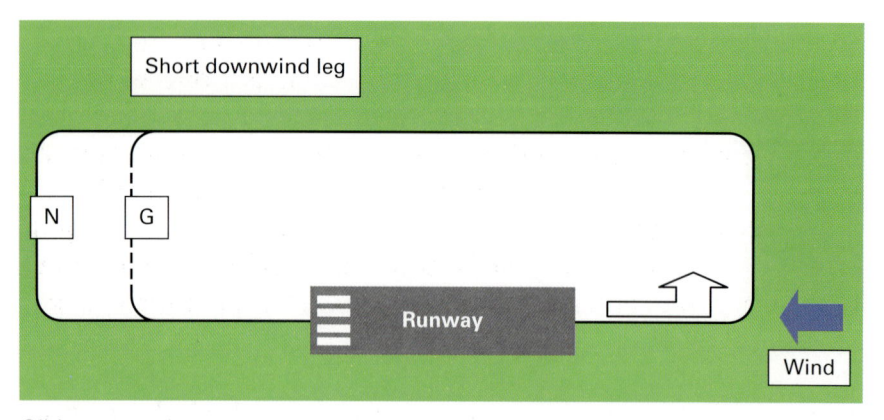

Glide approach.

THE BAD WEATHER CIRCUIT AND APPROACH

- Keep a very good lookout for other circuit traffic, as you are in a non-standard circuit.
- Be quick with the downwind calls and pre-landing checks as you are close in to the airfield (a good guide is to keep the wing tip travelling along/above the runway as you fly downwind) and it is an early turn onto base (about the same place as the glide, just at a lower altitude).
- The examiner will want you to be on the PAPIs – flying two red and two whites if available and working – so be proactive with the throttle to get on them as you turn onto final and stay on them as soon as possible and for as long as possible.

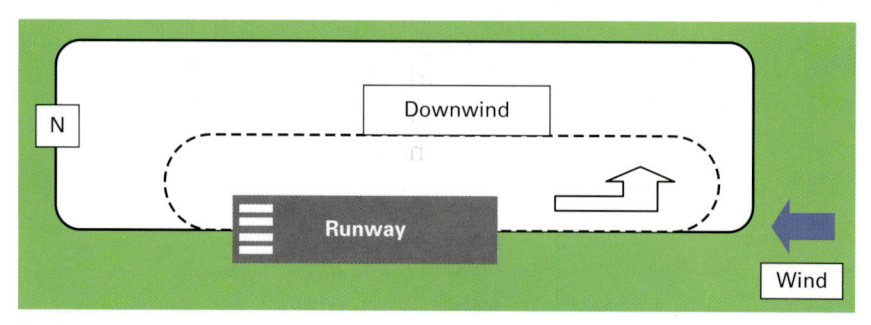

Bad-weather circuit.

It sounds obvious, but do remember to call out loud 'Reds, blues, three greens' at least once on final. No-one wants the humiliation of a gear-up landing – it makes a heck of a lot of noise, embarrassment and paperwork! In case you are unsure, this call means red lever fully forward (mixture control), blue lever fully forward (propeller control) and the three green lights are on confirming the gear is down and locked. If you don't have the three green lights, then you should initiate a go-around, depart the circuit just outside the ATZ and try to get the gear down and locked as per your emergency checklist. However, a few common reasons that you don't have those lights showing could be worth investigating:

- The bulb has blown – try swapping them around.
- The emergency gear lever has been pushed down accidently.
- The navigation lights have been turned on, causing the green lights to dim (which makes them look like they are off).
- The circuit breaker has popped.
- You forgot to put the gear down on downwind!

REJECTED TAKE-OFF

You will also be asked to do a rejected take-off. You will be asked to make a standard take-off run and the examiner will call out something before rotation speed that would or should cause you to abort the take-off, such as there is a horse running across the runway or you've had a bird strike. Close the throttle and stop the aircraft in as short a distance as possible while maintaining directional control. At the same time, pull the control column back as far as you can as it will assist in the braking action, and retract any flap you may have on as well. Obviously, you have right of way on the runway, but don't take too much time to stop and then vacate, especially if there is traffic on final.

GO-AROUNDS

If any of the approaches are unstable or you find that you will not be able to demonstrate the circuit that you have been asked to do, i.e. the runway is not clear, the best course of action is to execute a go-around.

Circuits

Show the examiner your good airmanship and decision-making skills by deciding early that you will need to go-around, give a brief explanation and then go for it. You will make the examiner nervous if it appears to him that you are trying to extend the glide because you have misjudged it, or that you are trying to land on a runway with traffic still on it. An early and safe decision is important.

So, the correct go-around procedure is:

1. Apply full power as you pitch the nose to a level attitude.
2. Remove the third stage of flap as the pitch attitude increases to a climb.
3. Wait for a positive rate of climb on the vertical speed indicator (VSI) before bringing the landing gear up.
4. Confirm a positive rate of climb to bring the second stage of flap up.
5. Confirm a positive rate of climb to bring the last stage of flap up.
6. Get the aircraft to Vy as soon as possible with the correct climb power settings.
7. Then and only then can you call a go-around on the radio.

Do not call the go-around on the radio until the aircraft is clean and climbing away. The priority is to get the aircraft climbing away from the ground as soon as possible and the radio call may distract you from the airspeed, which may have got critically close to the stall speed. This is even more important when you progress onto the multi-engine rating, as an asymmetric twin-engine aircraft with gear and full flap down struggles to climb away even on full power.

If you misjudge the approach and flare, or a gust of wind gets under the wing and you start to balloon, or even bounce and then balloon, you should execute the go-around procedure immediately. Don't forget to position yourself on the dead side as soon as you can.

FREDA CHECKS

Finally, remember to do FREDA checks every 15 minutes during the lesson and change the fuel tanks every 30 minutes, although they should be included in the pre-landing checks. See your own training notes or checklist for the aircraft-specific pre-landing checks.

JOINING THE AIRFIELD

As an aside to the circuit brief, we should also talk briefly about standard overhead joins. As an aspiring commercial pilot, we need to be making approaches to airfields that are as quick and direct as possible – time really is money in terms of fuel. This usually means that, if you have a choice, a direct-in or left- or right-base join should be the first option if it is safe. However, it is not always possible at some airfields or airports, which makes an overhead join necessary. As a general rule for a standard overhead join, it is overhead the threshold at 2,000ft, a descending turn on the dead side to be at circuit altitude overhead the upwind end of the runway. Then turn downwind at the normal place and continue as a normal circuit. Make a radio call stating that you are overhead, and as you join cross-wind and then make your standard downwind call. And it should go without saying that a good lookout is crucial. Don't say 'G-XXXX' is joining *for* runway 22L as it is a common mistake and implies the number four.

A left- or right-base join is a little more pressured, as you will need to have your airfield approach checks, pre-landing checks and radio calls done, as well as descending in time to be at circuit

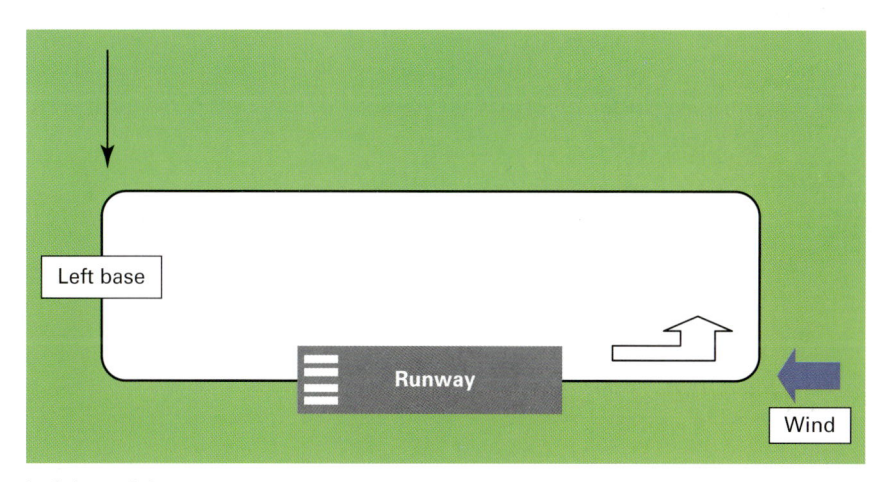

Left-base join.

altitude at left or right base ready to start your base configuration. Start these checks at about 10nm from the airfield to give yourself plenty of time to get it all done in good time. If you find that you have left the descent too late, or you have missed traffic on downwind and got too close to them, do not orbit in the ATZ: either turn the aircraft away before the ATZ or climb and position yourself safely overhead or onto the dead side of the circuit. Remember that traffic already in the circuit has right of way, so you must give way if required.

A direct join on final can be the most pressured join. You need to be configured to land with all your checks completed in good time, but not too early as you don't want to be on a long final at your final approach speed, which may mean a long wait until you get to the ground; it also means you need to be very wary of other traffic in the circuit and your positioning, so I would recommend a left- or right-base join over a direct approach on to final.

CROSS-WIND TECHNIQUES

Not demonstrating any or sufficient cross-wind take-off or landing technique will get the attention of the examiner ... and not in a good way. For take-off, you must put aileron into wind and use opposite rudder to keep the aircraft straight. For landing, in the flare, you must use opposite rudder to keep the nose straight and then put aileron into wind for the touchdown. That also goes for positioning in the circuit, as you will not maintain the correct track over the ground if you don't allow for the prevailing wind.

For different landing and take-off scenarios such as soft field you should consult the POH or your instructor for the exact procedure and speeds for your aircraft and airfield, and, should you be lucky enough to be at an airport that handles jet and or helicopter traffic, be very wary of wake turbulence!

> *Everyone already knows that the definition of a good landing is one you can walk away from. But very few know the definition of a great landing. It's one after which you can use the aircraft again.*
> *Anon.*

5 General Airwork

Learn from the mistakes of others. You won't live long enough to make them all yourself.

Anon.

This is probably the biggest section of the syllabus as it contains most of the manoeuvres you will do, including the stalls but not the emergencies; the latter are a separate section in the test, so are covered by Chapter 8. These manoeuvres should not be too difficult as most of them will have been covered in your PPL course, but the stalls and the steep gliding turn could be different to how you were originally taught. The correct procedure for all of the manoeuvres (to test standard naturally) is covered here for consistency and continuity.

If you see any traffic while looking out, use the clock code to point it out to the examiner, i.e. say 'traffic 3 o'clock high' rather than point and say 'I think there is something over there!'

> *Remember that the lookout before and after each manoeuvre is as important as the manoeuvre itself!*

ACCELERATION AND DECELERATION

You will be asked to accelerate to a particular airspeed, while maintaining heading and altitude. After a good lookout, you need to apply full power (leave the prop lever where it is), lowering the nose to maintain altitude and, when the ASI is reading the airspeed you want, reduce the power to maintain the requested speed and altitude. In the Piper Arrow, this is about 25in MP as the cruise setting is 22in MP. This should hold the airspeed you want while maintaining altitude. To recover back to the cruise, set the cruise power setting and allow the aircraft to decelerate to the cruise speed. (Obviously, if you are not flying in a Piper Arrow, you will need to get your instructor to advise you on appropriate power settings.)

You will then be asked to decelerate to a particular airspeed, again maintaining heading and altitude. The trick to this one is to reduce the power to quite a low setting such as 15in MP (leaving the prop lever where it is), maintain the altitude by pitching the nose up and, as the speed reduces to within 5kt of the desired airspeed, apply approximately 19in MP in the Piper Arrow. Trim and then adjust the power as required while maintaining the speed with the pitch attitude, and then the altitude with the throttle.

Always get the speed first with the pitch attitude and then get level flight using the throttle in this exercise, not the other way round.

VISUAL UNUSUAL ATTITUDES

The examiner will take control of the aircraft and put it into a steep descending turn. They will then ask you to take control and recover. The recovery is: close the throttle, roll the wings level and pitch the nose up to the horizon. As the airspeed reduces toward the cruise speed, feed the power back in to the cruise setting and maintain the altitude that you levelled off at.

30- AND 45-DEGREE ANGLE OF BANK TURNS

You shouldn't really need to be briefed on how to do a 30-degree angle of bank (AoB) turn so I will just remind you of the steep turn. Students often think that they need to do a HASELL or a FREDA check before a steep turn, but you don't. Just have a very good look out before you start and a very good lookout as you roll wings level out of the turn. So:

1. Roll into a 30-degree AoB turn and then promptly into the 45-degree AoB turn. The quicker you roll in, the easier it is to maintain altitude.
2. Once at the 45-degree AOB turn, apply back pressure to the control column and, if needed, feed 1in of manifold pressure in to help maintain the altitude.

3. Lookout in the direction of the turn, while using the visual horizon to maintain altitude.
4. Check the AI to make sure you are still at 45 degrees, then lookout.
5. Check the altimeter to make sure you are maintaining altitude, then lookout.
6. Check the balance ball to make sure you are still in balance, then lookout.
7. Check the DI/HSI to make sure you don't roll out past your nominated heading.
8. As you roll out on heading, release the back pressure and reduce the manifold pressure to cruise setting.

CLIMBING AND DESCENDING AT GIVEN SPEEDS AND RATE OF CLIMB/DESCENT

The examiner will ask you what speeds you will fly during the ground brief before the test, so make sure you know what Vx and Vy are. You will be asked to climb at either speed during the other manoeuvres so you probably won't be asked to do it as a separate exercise. The climb will be done with the standard power, attitude and trim. If the instructor asks you to descend at a certain rate of descent at cruise speed, as a guide if you reduce 1in of manifold pressure, you will descend at roughly 100fpm. You don't want to descend any quicker than 750fpm, as that is when eardrums start to pop and could cause your passengers some ear pain.

If, on your test, you find you have left it too late to descend for whatever reason, just explain to the examiner you need to expedite and if they feel any physical discomfort to tell you so you can increase the power slightly and reduce the rate of descent.

STEEP GLIDING TURNS

This is probably a manoeuvre that you haven't done before, so be careful with it. First, you need to put the aircraft in a glide. Close the throttle (the landing gear warning horn will go off, but you are allowed to ignore it), and trim for the best glide speed (80kt in the Piper Arrow). After a very good lookout, turn the aircraft into a 30-degree AOB descending turn and pitch very slightly

General Airwork

down to get to 85kt (don't pitch too far forward as the airspeed will very quickly increase). Hold the speed and the attitude for one second and then turn the aircraft into a 45-degree AOB descending turn. You want to achieve 90kt at 45 degrees but, as the aircraft is accelerating, you will actually need to pitch up to maintain the 90kt or else the airspeed will very quickly accelerate beyond 90kt. Hold that attitude for 1 second and then roll back to a 30-degree AOB turn while letting the airspeed reduce to 85kt, hold for 1 second and then roll back to wings level and the glide descent. Hold for 1 second and reset the cruise power to get back to the cruise speed.

You will lose a lot of height during this manoeuvre but as long as you recover at a reasonable height (i.e. before you get too close to the ground), there is no height loss requirement. You may also be asked to roll out on a certain heading, so be aware of the rate of turn and speed it up or slow it down as required, so you can roll out as requested.

STALLS

You will be asked to demonstrate three stall entries and recoveries: a clean stall, a base-to-final stall and a final stall.

The clean stall is the only stall you will be asked to do where you recover on the examiner's command, so don't try to pre-empt the recovery before they say so.

We start with a HASELL check:

H   Height is sufficient to recover: usually anything above 3,000ft agl.
A   Airframe: landing gear is up, flaps are up and brakes are off.
S   Security: hatches and harnesses are secure, there are no loose articles around the cockpit (as far as possible).
E   Engine: check that the temperatures and pressures are in the green, the mixture is rich and the fuel pump on.
L   Location: clear of airfields, built up areas, cloud, controlled airspace and danger areas (i.e. ABCCD).
L   Lookout: make either a 180-degree turn or two 90-degree turns and really look out, up and down as well as side to side.

Once you have finished the HASELL checks, put the aircraft into the stall configuration as soon as possible, otherwise the lookout you just did will need doing again. Once you have completed one full HASELL check before a stall, you can abbreviate the HASELL check to the HELL check on the subsequent stalls.

These stalls are meant to be flown with minimum height loss and a prompt recovery, and always a positive rate of climb in the recovery.

THE CLEAN STALL

Set the bug on your current heading, close the throttle (you should hear the landing gear warning horn go off – this is the only time it is acceptable to hear this) and pitch the nose up to maintain altitude. This will obviously cause the airspeed to reduce. In the Piper Arrow you will find that a continuous pitch-up will cause the aircraft to climb initially, so you need to pitch up a very small amount to the horizon and wait, pitch up and wait. Maintain the lookout while pitching up: you are recovering on the examiner's command, so you don't need to keep your eyes inside looking at the instruments.

Once you have been told to recover (this can be at any airspeed), it is pitch, power, roll and climb. Step by step this means: pitch the nose down to just below the visual horizon as you smoothly but promptly apply full power, roll the wings level (if necessary, which it shouldn't be) and pitch the nose up into a positive rate of climb, i.e. the climb attitude.

Set the climb power of 25in MP and leave the prop at 2,400rpm, and then let the aircraft accelerate to the best rate of climb speed while being very careful not to let the VSI show a rate of descent. You will need quite a big pitch-up nose attitude, so don't relax that back pressure.

Don't get fixated on the ASI – this is a common mistake. You are looking for a safe airspeed (i.e. increasing) and a positive rate of climb, and only then do you look to the ASI for Vy. Hold the nose attitude for Vy for approximately 3 seconds and then level off while looking out. Return the MP to 22in as the airspeed reaches cruise speed and lookout again wing tip to wing tip.

General Airwork

THE BASE TO FINAL STALL

This exercise is intended to create a scenario where you are configured on the base leg in the circuit, you turn on to the final approach but get distracted and there is an inadvertent pitch-up that results in the stall warning horn going off. You are actually meant to recover at the first sign of the stall in this exercise, so be aware that it may be the stall warning horn but it may also be some buffeting so be prepared to recover at either.

Make sure you do a HASELL/HELL check first. Then, set the aircraft up for base. Reduce the power to approximately 12in MP (it is usually 17in MP on base but we won't get the aircraft to stall with all that power on), check the airspeed is within the landing gear limits for extension (129kt), bring the landing gear down and then smoothly apply the first and second stages of flap. Keep the nose up to the horizon to maintain the altitude until you reach your base speed and then pitch the nose down to maintain it. Lookout either left or right and turn sensibly if not instructed which way to go (i.e. away from anything mentioned in the location part of the HASELL checks).

You are now in a 20-degree AOB descending turn, so immediately pitch up to maintain altitude, while still turning, looking in the direction of the turn and wait for the first sign of the stall. If the stall warning horn or the buffet is not felt after about 10 seconds, reduce the MP to approximately 11in. Initiate the recovery at the first sign; as before, the recovery is pitch, power, roll and climb. Pitch down to just below the visual horizon as you smoothly but promptly apply full power, roll the wings level and pitch the nose up into a large positive rate of climb. Keep the aircraft in balance in the climb.

As soon as you have a positive rate of climb on the VSI, call it out and bring the landing gear up. Then, as you keep pitching up to maintain the positive rate of climb, bring the second stage of flap up and then, again maintaining the positive rate of climb, bring the first stage of flap up. Keeping the nose held at the climb attitude, set the climb power and leave the prop at 2,400rpm. Then let the aircraft accelerate to the best rate of climb speed while being very careful not to let the VSI show a rate of descent.

General Airwork

Don't get fixated on the ASI. You are looking for a safe airspeed (i.e. increasing) and a positive rate of climb, and only then do you look to the ASI for Vy. Remember that it is a big pitch-up moment, so don't relax the back pressure. Hold the nose attitude for Vy for approximately 3 seconds and then level off while looking out. Return the MP to cruitse setting as the airspeed reaches cruise speed and look out again, wing tip to wing tip.

> **HASELL Checks:**
> H = height
> A = airframe
> S = security
> E = engine
> L = location
> L = lookout

THE FINAL APPROACH STALL

This is to recreate a scenario where you are configured on the final approach in the circuit but get distracted and there is an inadvertent pitch-up that results in the stall warning horn going off. As with the base to final stall, note that you are actually meant to recover at the first sign of the stall in this exercise, whether it is the stall warning horn or some buffeting, so be prepared to recover at either (depending on the aircraft type you are flying).

Make sure you do a HASELL/HELL check first. Then, set the aircraft up for the final approach. Reduce the MP to approximately 12in, check the airspeed is within

> *Note: all these power settings and speeds are accurate for the Piper Arrow, so if you are flying another aircraft type, amend them as per your instructor's instructions or what is recommended in the aircraft's POH.*

the landing gear extension limits, bring the landing gear down and then smoothly apply the first, second and then final stages of flap. Keep the nose up to maintain the altitude until you reach your base speed and then pitch the nose down to maintain that speed.

General Airwork

Pitch up to maintain altitude (and maintain heading with ailerons neutral and rudder), and wait for the first sign of the stall. If the stall warning horn or the buffet is not felt after about 10 seconds, then reduce the MP to 11in. Initiate the recovery at the first sign: pitch, power, roll and climb.

As soon as you have applied full power, bring the drag flap up as soon as possible – you don't need a positive rate of climb to bring the drag flap up. Then wait for a positive rate of climb on the VSI, call it out and bring the landing gear up. As you keep pitching up to maintain the positive rate of climb, bring the second and first stages of flap up. Keeping in the climbing attitude, set the prop and power levers for climb, and then let the aircraft accelerate to the best rate of climb while being very careful not to let the VSI show a rate of descent. Keep the aircraft in balance.

As with the other two stalls, don't get fixated on the ASI. You are looking for a safe airspeed (i.e. increasing) and a positive rate of climb, and only then do you look to the ASI for Vy. Remember the pitch-up to the climbing attitude needed to maintain the positive rate of climb. Hold the nose attitude for Vy for approximately 3 seconds and then level off while looking out. Return the MP to cruise setting as the airspeed reaches cruise speed, and look out again wing tip to wing tip.

You must keep the ailerons level during the stall entry and recovery in the clean and final stall, and it is a potential fail point if you use them on the entry or roll the aircraft level before pitching and applying full power in the recovery. You must apply a good dose of right rudder when you have climb power set, as you will be reprimanded in the debrief if the aircraft is out of balance in the climb. There is a list of common fail points and mistakes that have been made by previous students doing these exercises at the end of this book.

6 Instrument Flying

It's best to keep the pointed end going forward as much as possible.
Anon.

As explained in the Introduction, there is a minimum of 10 hours instrument flying that needs to be done by you as part of the 25-hour course. This may seem like a lot for a VFR licence, but the reason for so many IF hours is safety. You and your passengers need to be safe in case flight in IMC becomes unavoidable. Some of the manoeuvres you will be demonstrating are with the full instrument panel available to you and some are called limited panel: they must be done without reference to the AI and HSI.

We can simulate flight in cloud in the aircraft by the student wearing foggles. These are very tasteful large plastic glasses that you wear on your head; the top of the lens is 'fogged' out but you can see the instruments. Alternatively, we can place plastic screens up and around the cockpit so you can't see outside but – a small but important point I think! – the examiner can.

Be aware that you may also do some of your flying in 'real' cloud, as you can't really simulate the unpleasant physical sensations of flying in cloud.

If your ATO has access to an approved simulator, you can do a maximum of 5 hours of instrument flying in it; this allows us to get your instrument flying scan and skills and procedures up to test standard before getting into the aircraft. It allows the instructor to pause, talk through any training issues and re-start the lesson as required, which can be useful but which is obviously not really an option in the aircraft.

Spend some time on your own, in the aircraft and on the ground on a bad weather day, so you can become proficient at putting them up.

Instrument Flying

> **Top Tip**
>
> It is wise to make sure you are proficient at putting the screens up in the aircraft, as they can be a little awkward in a small cockpit – you don't want to knock the examiner around the head as you put them up.

The first thing you will need to do is learn the IF checks as you will be expected to repeat them to your instructor or examiner once you are in simulated instrument flying conditions. Remember that these also need to be repeated whether you are flying in the simulator or actually enter cloud during your test (though only in the IF section as you shouldn't be entering cloud on the rest of the skill test...). Be sure to read all the IF checks out by saying something like 'I would..., I could...', and be prepared to actually do some of the things you say.

The IF checks I use are:

1. Check the pitot heat is on.
2. Check the wings for ice – actual or simulated.
3. Climb or descend to MSA – make sure you know how to calculate it.
4. Execute a 180-degree turn.
5. Upgrade to traffic service.
6. Request radar vectors to visual, i.e around the cloud.
7. Ask for a surveillance radar approach.

To avoid overloading you with work, your examiner will be responsible for navigation, ATC liaison, the lookout and collision avoidance while you are flying with the screens up. However, you will be expected to ask the examiner if it is clear to turn before you do, so that they can have a good lookout for real. (And you are still responsible for FREDA checks.)

When instrument flying, the instrument scan radiates out from the AI to the HSI, back to the AI, to the altimeter back to the AI, to the ASI and back to the AI and then occasionally down to the turn co-ordinator, to the AI, down to the VSI and back to the AI.

Instrument Flying

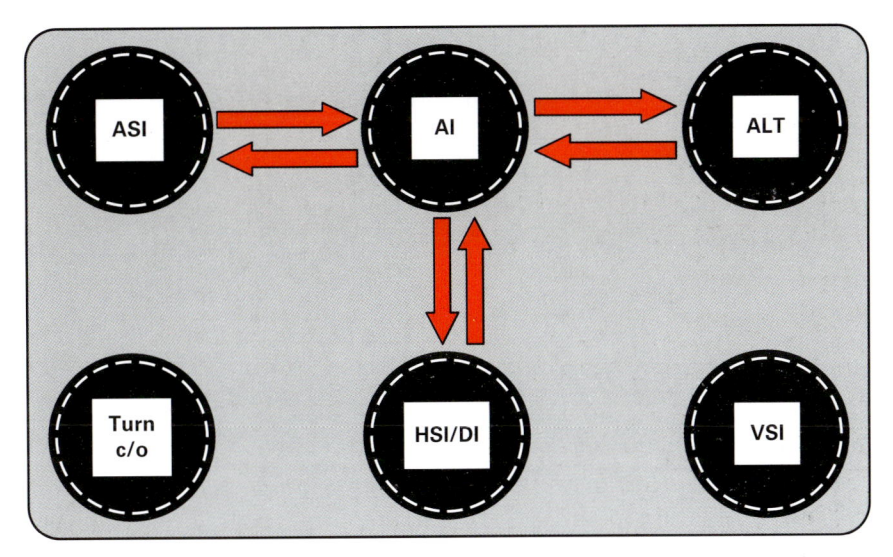

Basic full-panel 'T' scan.

Remember that as with visual flying, you need to fly attitudes on the AI while under the screens, or you will struggle with maintaining heading and altitude. You probably haven't flown on instruments since the PPL and so you may take a little time to settle into it. Remember – the AI is your primary instrument and you look at the wings and the dot between them, not the sky pointer at the top of the AI. Also, staring at one instrument at a time is a common thing to do and it will cause you problems – you need a smooth, continuous scan of all the instruments as shown above.

It is not uncommon for students to feel disorientated during the first couple of IF lessons. It may seem that the instruments are telling you one thing but your body is telling you another. You must believe the instruments, no matter how uncomfortable or 'odd' you may feel. Trust the instruments and if you still feel uneasy, check that the vacuum gauge is still reading positively, which should allow you to trust them. The other trick is to make small, gentle inputs into the controls and return to a straight and level attitude if you feel out of control.

So, back to the actual flying: you will be asked to fly the following manoeuvres with the full panel available.

ACCELERATION AND DECELERATION

You will be asked to accelerate/decelerate to a nominated airspeed, maintaining heading and altitude. The procedure for both is no different from how you would do it in visual flight conditions – you are just using the AI instead of the outside horizon. Remember though to fly an attitude first, then get the nominated airspeed, and then use the throttle to maintain altitude. Speed first, then altitude is the key.

A RATE ONE TURN AND A 30-DEGREE AOB TURN

This is the way the examiner will see if your scan is really good enough: you will need to maintain a rate one (approximately 17 degrees AoB in a Piper Arrow) or a 30-degree AoB turn, maintaining altitude and rolling out on a desired heading. The procedure is the same for visual flying, but remember that you may have to pitch up a very small amount (if at all) for the steep turn to maintain altitude.

CLIMBING AND DESCENDING

The procedure is the same for visual flying; in the climb, it is still power, attitude (approximately 8 degrees pitch up in the Piper Arrow for 90kt) and trim, and be reasonably quick to get that pitch-up attitude.

If you are asked to descend at a certain rate of descent, remember that it is approximately 1in MP off for every 100fpm you want to descend. Again, get the speed first and then adjust the throttle to get the rate of descent that you have been asked to fly. The pitch attitude for 500fpm can be achieved by putting the top of the ball just underneath the horizon line as you reduce the power. The most common mistake is probably students moving the control column too far down too quickly.

POSITION FIX

You could be asked to do a position fix using one VOR and DME. You will need to tune and identify

Don't forget to do those FREDA checks

the VOR and DME before using them as it is a fail point if you don't. You then centre the needle with a 'from' flag and draw a line on your map out from the centre of the VOR. Be careful to draw the line from the correct VOR, and the correct radial – getting these wrong are common mistakes. You need to be really accurate or you will get an inaccurate position fix. Be quick though with drawing the line: steer with your feet if you have to take your hands off the controls. You then need to read off the DME distance, put your ruler on the line you have drawn and draw a circle about the size of a 5p piece around the distance shown on the DME. A successful position fix should mean that you are somewhere in that circle. Double check that the CDI needle is still centred before giving the examiner your position, or else re-do it. Also allow for the fact that you are travelling forward and your DME distance may be increasing or decreasing as you plot your position. Make sure the aircraft is trimmed correctly so when you take your hands off the controls, the aircraft doesn't wander too far away from heading and altitude.

LIMITED PANEL – TIMED TURNS AND UNUSUAL ATTITUDE RECOVERY

The limited panel flying may seem a little daunting but it is surprising how easy it becomes if you relax and make small gentle inputs. The scan for the limited panel flying is obviously different to the scan for the full panel as you are now simulating a suction pump failure and so you are without a fully functioning AI and HSI. So the scan for limited panel is as shown below your primary instrument is now the turn co-ordinator.

You will also be asked to do a compass turn and recovery from various unusual attitudes on limited panel.

Timed Turn
A successful 'timed' turn is all down to accuracy and timing. Make sure again that the aircraft is trimmed for straight and level, then look at the compass for the heading you are currently flying and put that heading on the ADF or VOR 2. Next, calculate the number of seconds it will take to get onto the heading the instructor or examiner has asked for.

Instrument Flying

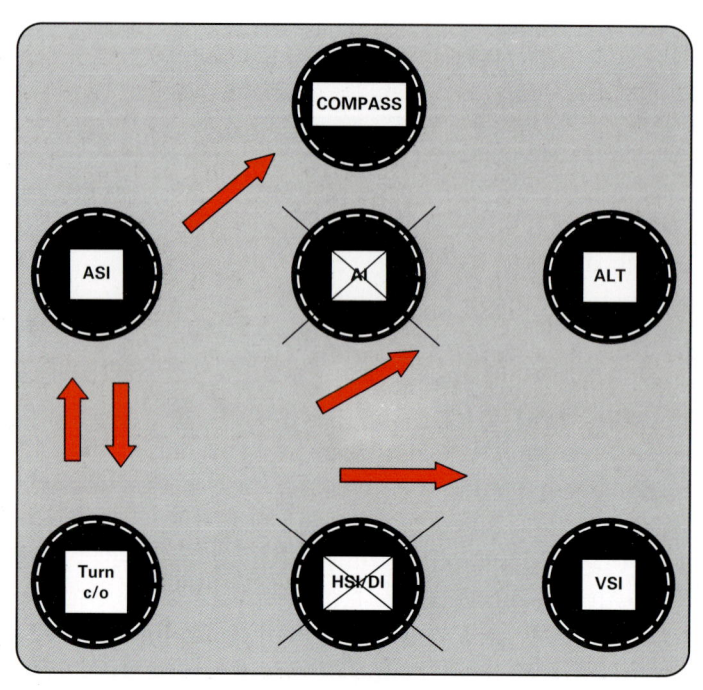

Limited panel scan from the turn co-ordinator.

For example: it takes 10 seconds to turn 30 degrees in a rate one turn and 3 seconds for 10 degrees. So if you are heading 180 degrees and you are asked to turn onto 270, look at the ADF or VOR, noting that it must be a turn to the right and will take 30 seconds. (A turn in the wrong direction is a fail, so be sure to check which way to turn.) Then go back to the compass and double check that you are still heading 180 degrees. If so, great news. If not, then re-set the heading on the ADF or VOR2 to the one you are now on and re-calculate the number of seconds. The procedure is the same if the stopwatch doesn't start or you forget to set it going: just roll the wings level, look at the compass heading once it has settled down and re-calculate the number of seconds needed to get to the heading you were asked for.

Then, promptly enter a rate one turn (approximately 18 degrees in an Arrow) and halfway through

Don't forget a FREDA check and to change fuel tanks during this exercise.

initiating the turn, start the stopwatch. (Do make sure the stopwatch is wound up and working before you start!) Once the stopwatch shows 30 seconds, don't turn the stop watch off, just start to roll out of the turn at the same speed that you rolled into the turn. (If you try to stop the stopwatch and then roll out, you will overshoot.)

Remain straight and level for a few seconds to allow the compass to settle and then look at it. Hopefully, you will be showing the heading you were asked for. If you are within 5 degrees then that is fine. If, however, the heading you rolled out on is greater than 5 degrees out, you will need to use the same method to get to the heading you were asked for. Don't wait for the examiner to prompt you, just do it. They will be tolerant if it takes you a couple of goes, but you should get it within two attempts or else they may ask you to do it again.

UNUSUAL ATTITUDE RECOVERY

The examiner will take control of the aircraft and they will put it into an unusual attitude as described below. They will then say 'Recover' and you must return the aircraft to straight and level flight in a smooth and reasonably prompt manner. The descriptions below may sound somewhat scary but it is actually easier to do than you think.

Neither the power setting nor the trim will be adjusted by the examiner, so if you relax the flying controls into a 'neutral' position at the end of the recovery then you won't be too far away from straight and level, and then you can make small adjustments to get yourself back to level flight.

Steep Climbing Turn

The examiner will take control of the aircraft once the AI and HSI have been covered and they will put the aircraft into a steep climbing turn. They will then ask you to recover. You must recover quickly but always in the correct order, otherwise it is a fail point.

You must look at the ASI first as that will decide your initial action. The airspeed should be reducing so you must apply full power. As you do so, look at the turn co-ordinator and roll wings

Instrument Flying

level. To get the aircraft straight and level, you must actually roll the aircraft through level flight to the rate one marker on the other side before rolling back level. It sounds odd but this will get you wings level in the quickest way.

Lastly, look at the altimeter and VSI as they should be showing a (usually reducing) rate of climb and increase in altitude. Relax (do not push forward!) the control column into the neutral position. If you push the smallest amount too far forward on the control column, you will pitch through level flight into a descent, which then makes it so much harder to get back to level flight. This is called 'flying the wavy navy', as you are constantly pushing and pulling on the control column. If you do start to over-control, remember to just relax the grip on the controls, relax your arms and neutralize the control column. Immediately restart your limited panel scan out from the turn co-ordinator to maintain level flight.

Steep Descending Turn
The examiner will also put the aircraft into a steep descending turn. They will then ask you to recover. As above, you must recover quickly but always in the correct order otherwise it is a fail point.

You must look at the ASI first as that will decide your initial action. The airspeed should be increasing so you must close the throttle completely. (The undercarriage warning horn may go off, but you can ignore it for this exercise.) As you do so, look at the turn co-ordinator and roll wings level. As above, to get the aircraft straight and level, you must roll the aircraft through level flight to the rate one marker on the other side before rolling back level.

Lastly, look at the altimeter and VSI as they should be showing a (usually increasing) rate of descent and decrease in altitude. Relax (don't pull back too aggressively) the control column into the neutral position. If you pull the nose up too far on the control column, you will pitch through level flight into a climb, which then makes it so much harder to get back to level flight. It's back to the 'flying the wavy navy' as you are constantly pushing and pulling on the control column. If you so start to over-control, remember to just relax the grip on the controls, relax your arms and neutralize the control column. Immediately restart your limited panel scan out from the turn co-ordinator to maintain level flight.

Steep Turn
This is the last manoeuvre in the limited panel unusual attitude section. The examiner will put the aircraft into a steep turn. They will then ask you to recover. As above, you must recover quickly but always in the correct order otherwise it is a fail point.

You must immediately look at the ASI first as that will decide your initial action. The airspeed should be steady at just less than your cruise speed. If it is increasing or decreasing as a trend, then it isn't a steep turn. The recovery then is to leave the throttle alone. So, look at the turn co-ordinator and roll wings level in the opposite direction of the turn. As above, to get the aircraft straight and level, you must roll the aircraft through level flight to the rate one marker on the other side before rolling back level.

Lastly, look at the altimeter and VSI as they should be showing a constant altitude. If not, then relax the control column into the neutral position. Remember that if you pitch the nose up too far (or down for that matter) on the control column, you will pitch through level flight into a climb then a descent which then makes it so much harder to get back to level flight. It's back to the 'flying the wavy navy' as you are constantly pushing and pulling on the control column. If you so start to over-control, remember to just relax the grip on the controls, relax your arms and neutralize the control column. Immediately restart your limited panel scan out from the turn co-ordinator to maintain level flight.

THE INSTRUMENT PROCEDURE

This has to be done as part of the CPL syllabus but it is not usually tested, so I won't go into any specifics here. You might fly one or two procedures in the simulator rather than in the aircraft, but these will be briefed by your instructor.

As far as the radio navigation aids go, you will have to tune, identify and test them all on the ground before take-off. However, they must also be tuned and identified prior to use in the air, or it is a fail point in the skill test. You can either learn Morse code

Instrument Flying

or, if you don't know it, write down the Morse ident for all the navigation aids that you may use. Remember that you can't use them while on the initial leg of your navigation but you can on the diversion, so you will need to make notes of the idents of navigation aids that may be useful to you. Also, make sure you also know or write down the Morse ident for TST as that is the ident you will hear if the navigation aid is unserviceable. They are usually NOTAM'd if the navigation aid is out. You can use GPS (if installed) if no other navigation aids are available for the position fix, but it can be used for range and bearing only. There has been an instance of an examiner asking a student to use the 'go-to' function on the GPS to get a direct track to a place to start a navigation exercise from, as the planned initial route became unflyable, so make sure you can at least use this function on it.

ADF/NDB TRACKING

NDBs should provide bearings accurate to within +/−5 degrees and the range depends on the transmission power, frequency and weather conditions. The range can be found in the AIP ENR 4-1-1. RBIs are fixed-card displays: you can move the card with the compass headings on it by hand and it will not move as the aircraft changes heading, whereas RMIs are rotating card displays that show the same heading as the aircraft's DI/HSI. You will have to identify which is installed in the aircraft you are flying.

One way to remember how to track QDMs (magnetic bearing to the beacon) is:

- needle more, steer more
- needle less, steer less

What this means in practice is that if the needle is pointing to a QDM more than you want (numerically), you will need to steer the aircraft 30 degrees more than the QDM you want; that allows for a 30-degree intercept. Once the head of the needle is pointing to the QDM you want, steer the aircraft onto that QDM, plus or minus the drift.

So, if the needle is pointing to a QDM less than you want (numerically) you will need to steer the aircraft 30 degrees less than the QDM you want, for a 30-degree intercept. Once the head of the needle is pointing to the QDM you want, steer the aircraft on to that QDM, plus or minus the drift.

To track QDRs (magnetic bearing from the beacon) is the opposite to the QDM method:

- needle more, steer less
- needle less, steer more

Therefore, if the needle is pointing to a QDR more than you want (numerically), you will need to steer the aircraft 30 degrees less than the QDR you want, which allows for a 30-degree intercept. Once the tail of the needle is pointing to the QDR you want, steer the aircraft on to that QDR, plus or minus the drift.

So, if the needle is pointing to a QDR less than you want (numerically), you will need to steer the aircraft 30 degrees more than the QDR you want, for a 30-degree intercept. Once the tail of the needle is pointing to the QDR you want, steer the aircraft on to that QDR, plus or minus the drift.

There are various methods of intercepting and tracking NDBs and I have found this one the easiest to remember and apply. You may well have been taught a different method already and be happy to use that one, but you must make sure you are 100 per cent happy with whichever method you use, as if you start to mix the various methods for NDB tracking, you will get yourself in a muddle, which could result in you turning the wrong way. I strongly recommend you buy a copy of RANT XL (an instrument trainer for use on a home computer) or something similar so that you can practise these at home. It is much cheaper to buy it and practise tracking until you are competent at home, than to keep doing them in the simulator or in the aircraft.

> ### Top Tip
> The ADF needle suffers from 'dip' and so is not accurate in a turn. You will be taught about 'dip' and how to interpret the needle in the turn once you start the instrument rating.

VOR INTERCEPTING AND TRACKING

There are usually two VORs installed in the aircraft and they should have an accuracy of +/−2 degrees if working normally. The VOR needle is the CDI needle on an HSI and 1 dot is 2 degrees deviation, so 10 degrees off is 5 dots as indicated on the VOR.

You will be asked to intercept and track a radial to or from a VOR, so remember to tune and identify it before you use it as it is a fail point. Also, immediately identify any co-located DME as well as it is a good habit to get into.

You should select the radial on NAV 1 and establish whether it is a fly left or right indication. If you have a full-scale deflection to the left (or right) you will need to use a 30-degree intercept. Subtract (or add) 30 degrees from the radial you have been asked to intercept and that is your new aircraft heading.

Establish yourself on that heading as soon as you can and be aware when the CDI needle starts to move towards the centre. Once it is within 1–2 degrees of the centre, turn the aircraft onto the radial, plus or minus the drift. What the examiner is looking for is that you are flying a sensible heading that will keep the CDI needle centred, allowing for the wind correction.

> **Top Tip**
>
> Use the max drift rule to make a sensible guess (or use the windstar from your navigation leg for a really accurate drift adjustment.)

Have a look at the DME distance: make yourself think about how quickly that needle may move, as obviously the closer you are to the beacon, the quicker it will move and it is very easy to overshoot the centre. If you are far away from the beacon and the needle isn't moving within a minute or so, you can increase the intercept angle to 60 degrees: you change the aircraft heading by a further 30 degrees so you can get on to the radial as soon as you can, and it is an acceptable way of speeding the procedure up.

Instrument Flying

Lastly, there is also a possibility that the examiner will ask you what you would do if the engine were to cut out while you are under the screens. What they are looking for you to say is that you would trim the aircraft for the best glide speed, establish your position by whatever means you have available, look at your MSA and hope that when you break cloud, you will be able to make a safe landing in a field.

The FNPT II simulator used by CPL students at Stapleford Flight Centre.

7 Navigation

Airspeed, altitude or brains: two are always needed to successfully complete the flight.

Anon.

The navigation exercise in the CPL is only a little different from that taught in PPL navigation. There are no flight plans the first leg is just you, a plog, a chart and a watch.

A CPL navigation route is one planned leg only with the en-route diversion planned while in the air. You may or may not get to your original destination before you are asked to divert somewhere else, as it is at the instructor's or examiner's discretion. Be prepared for a diversion from the half-way point onwards.

The original destination and the diversion point can be a small airfield (used or disused), a small town, a ground feature or similar. This is professional flying now, so expect some difficult places to find – the instructors deliberately make you take us to small, disused airfields, so if you get a smallish town or village on your test, it will make the navigation seem a lot easier.

So, the first thing to is make sure your map is up to date (use the latest 1:500,000 issued by the CAA) and make sure you keep the yellow card that comes with the chart with the frequencies and other information on it, as this is very useful for telling what kind of service the airfields can or can't give you. This is even more important if you haven't flown in UK airspace before.

Don't forget that you are being tested on airmanship, RT, potential icing conditions, safety and and use of checklists, as well as navigation.

PLANNING YOUR NAVIGATION

As for planning your navigation, you will need to study your route carefully and take your time planning so there are no nasty surprises once you are in the air. As a student commercial pilot, you should be able to fill this in without any help from your instructor.

Navigation

Navigation planning.

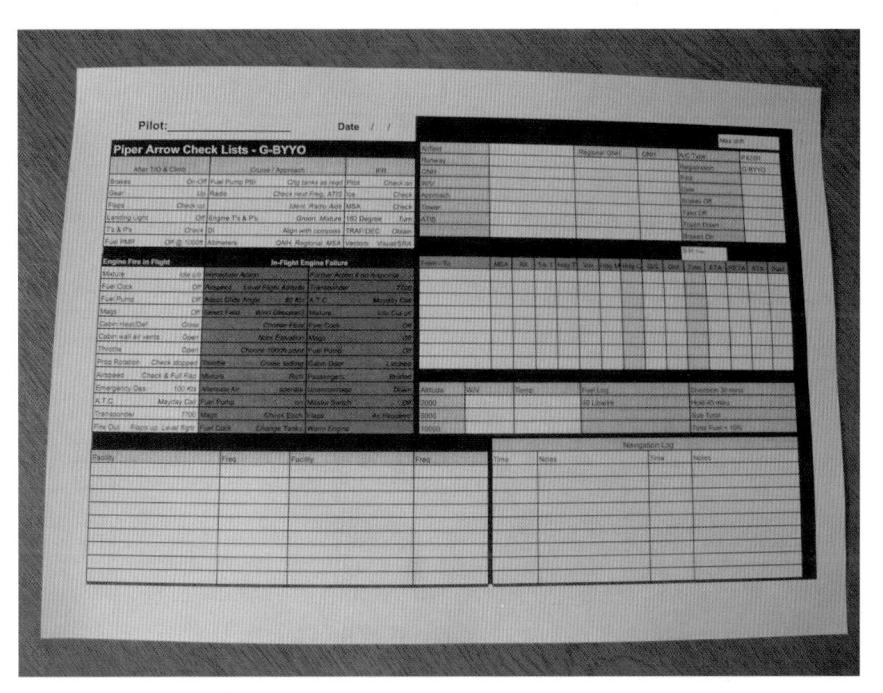

An example of a CPL plog.

Navigation

Everyone has a slightly different way of planning a navigation, as well as dealing with any issues of being off-track and planning a diversion while in the air, so use my method or that which your instructor tells you.

As a commercial pilot, you want to go the most direct route from A to B, as time is money in aviation. However, that doesn't mean you can go through controlled airspace, danger areas and such like if you aren't allowed to. You will also need to avoid glider sites and other potential hazardous areas, so if you have to plan a route that – as the crow flies – would go through such an area, plan a small diversion around it or extend the route so you don't get within 5 nautical miles of it. It can't be emphasized enough how dangerous it can be to fly near glider sites or parachute drop zones.

A service from a MATZ is obviously available during the published hours, but there can also be a service available outside of those hours so don't be afraid to ask. If you call up and get no reply, try again. If there is still no reply, you may continue but keep a listening watch and make position reports. You must try to call them early enough to get permission to transit through the MATZ and certainly any ATZs that may be lurking within the MATZ.

You should use a LARS when flying outside controlled airspace and certainly when there are no local airfields or airports within 25 nm that can offer you a service. They are normally available Monday to Friday, 08.00–17.00 local but many are often open twenty-four hours a day, so if in doubt, check before you leave the ground or call them once airborne.

Make sure you plan and have available the most sensible frequencies for the stations you want to talk to. It should be just as important as the planning of the navigation, so make sure of the correct station type, name and what kind of service they can offer. Asking for a basic service from an air/ground station is a big mistake as it shows that you have not done your planning properly. Also, if you pass within 5 nautical miles of an ATZ you must talk to that station regardless, but you also need to balance the needs of getting the service that will be the most use to you and potentially able to offer you some sort of radar service if the weather deteriorates, e.g. Farnborough radar, against getting

Navigation

local traffic information from a local station, e.g. Headcorn/ Lashenden radio.

Don't speak to any more stations than you need to, as it makes your workload so much harder, but then again, do make sure you are always in contact with someone in case of an emergency. Don't leave a long pause between leaving one frequency and talking on another; leave it any longer than two minutes between talking to someone and getting a service, and it becomes a fail point. Have a look at the chapter on RT Phrases and ATC services for examples of radio calls at the back of the book.

Note that you may have to request the regional QNHs for the various altimeter setting regions (ASRs) you pass through during the navigation, so have a frequency in mind for that before you take off. Don't forget to set the new regional QNH if you cross an ASR whilst on frequency to an Information or a LARS. It is in some ways easier to speak to local stations who can give you a local QNH, which then means that you may not need to set the regional pressure settings. I can't advise exactly which way is the best as it depends on the route you have been given to fly, so make a sensible decision: do you stay with an Information Service that will cover you for most of the route but will necessitate one or two regional pressure settings changes, or do you talk to potentially lots of local stations en route but using their QNH, which will be valid? It is so easy to forget to set the regional QNH, so if you make calls to local stations within 25nm of your track this will resolve this problem. Draw a line on the map where the boundary is, or write it on your plog to make sure you remember, as it is a fail if you enter an ASR without the correct QNH. At Stapleford, we request the London, Chatham and Yarmouth QNHs as we depart but obviously, if you are doing your training in other parts of the UK, be advised by your instructor on the ASRs and the QNHs you should set.

Be aware that you aren't allowed to use any navigational aids on the first leg to help confirm your position. Therefore, break the first leg down into either one waypoint in the middle or one each in the middle and at the quarter-way and three-quarter-way points. This then helps with the track error correction method that is described later. Don't divide the track into thirds, as the track error method that I describe won't work, and don't

67

Navigation

divide the track up over features, as that is a PPL habit and you now need to adopt professional practices.

Remember that you are not obliged to use this book's method of navigation, as the examiner just wants you to get to the requested destination safely and on time with a 'method', rather than just 'feature crawling' (navigating with reference to ground features alone). If you are happy with the way you were taught at PPL level, then use that method.

The examiner needs to see you using the chart, the ground features and your watch. If you see that you are off-track, then you make a track error adjustment, telling the examiner what you are doing. What they don't want to hear you say is, for example, 'I should be to the left of the reservoir in the distance so I am going to turn left a bit.' What you should say is something like 'I believe I am 10 degrees off track because I should be the left of X and to the right of Y, so I will double the error and make a new heading of XXX degrees that will take me to my destination and I will continue with my ETA of Z.' Or something similar. Just keep the examiner involved and updated so they don't think you are making random heading adjustments.

NAVIGATION – FIRST LEG

Once you have reached your starting point or set heading point, regardless of what or where it is, you will need to do the following checks:

1. Time
2. Turn
3. Talk
4. Gross Error Check
5. FREDA

You also need to do them at every waypoint. To expand on those checks:

Time – you need to write your set heading time down on your plog (the time you started the navigation exercise) and then calculate the ETA and write it down.

Navigation

- **Turn** – you need to turn onto your calculated heading and then adjust the DI/HSI against the compass so it is as accurate as possible. Note that even slaved units can and do go out of alignment, so always assume the DI/HSI is wrong and check it every few minutes.
- **Talk** – you will need to request a frequency change to your next en route frequency or set up the next frequency ready or make a radio call.
- **Gross Error Check** – you should to pick two large ground features, one to the left and one to the right to confirm that you are on the correct track and you aren't flying your groundspeed or your distance by mistake. For example, 'I am expecting to see a large reservoir to my right and a large town on my left.'
- **FREDA** – these should have been learnt as your cruise checks during your PPL, but if you need to refresh yourself, they are printed in full in your aircraft checklist.

> *Be wary of QNH changes – make sure you set them, either as you receive it as part of a service, or as you cross ASRs*

Once you have done that, you need to bring your attention back in full to the job of navigating. Look ahead, point out towns, villages, airfields (active and disused) and large ground features to keep yourself mentally ahead of the aircraft. However, don't guess – if you are not sure what the town is, keep quiet until you can confirm it by using three ground features to prove it to yourself and the examiner. The worst thing you can do on a navigation exercise is to mis-identify a town or feature, so help yourself by saying 'I believe that is X' and give yourself three reasons why, rather than saying it is somewhere with no evidence and so getting it wrong.

As you approach your first waypoint, think ahead to your Time–Turn–Talk–Gross Error–FREDA checks. In other words, anticipate your waypoints with reasons why you are approaching them; whether you are off track and will therefore have to make a heading change once you are there, and whether you will need to make an adjustment to the ETA. Pointing out large towns and features as you go along will force you to keep ahead

Navigation

of yourself and reassure you where you are. Don't be afraid to do all these out loud ... BUT, if you are unsure (or have even the slightest bit of doubt) do not positively identify any town: any misidentification could result in a fail as it implies that you are unsure of your position.

MAKING OFF-TRACK ADJUSTMENTS

You can make a heading adjustment at your quarter-way point by taking the number of degrees off track and multiplying it by 1.5. This will get you to your destination, but not back on track. You can make a heading adjustment at your halfway point by taking the number of degrees off track and multiplying it by 2. This will get you to your destination not back on track. You can make a heading adjustment at your three-quarter-way point by taking the number of degrees off track and multiplying it by 3. This will get you to your destination not back on track.

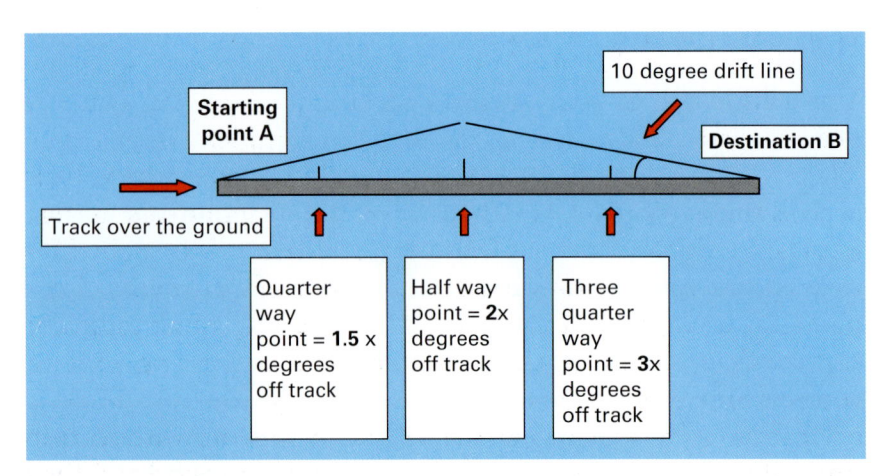

Off-track adjustment.

OTHER USEFUL NAVIGATION TECHNIQUES

Fly your planned headings and altitude accurately, and check that the DI/HSI and compass are aligned every few minutes as well as during your FREDA checks. Most track errors are caused by problems with this. Map-read carefully – don't make the mistake of saying the names of towns without careful

Navigation

thought and have at least three reasons to back your argument as to why they are what you say they are. Remember, there is always time to think before you need to speak. Keep your plog going with accurate ETAs, ATAs, heading and altitude changes, and expected fuel consumption. Make a note of any discrepancies. Don't change heading without a very good reason. Avoid panicky,

> **Remember to perform a FREDA check as a minimum every 30 minutes.**

ill-thought-out changes. Apply as accurate as possible a procedure for a new heading and explain out loud how you have come to this new heading. Remember that there is absolutely no feature-crawling or using radio aids on first leg. You may not orbit at your destination, but you can on your diversion leg as well as using any radio aids available.

DIVERSION PLANNING

You will be told at some point on the original leg that you will need to plan a diversion for a reason the examiner will give you. The reason is obviously not real, but will be reasonably realistic such as the weather having closed in or the airfield that you were hoping to land at having closed due to runway incursion. You may be told this during the first leg or as you get to your destination. Be prepared to be given the diversion route after the halfway point, but don't be too distracted by worrying about it before it happens.

Once you get your diversion, if you have time without too much distraction, first draw the track over the ground and then look up and check your heading and altitude. Get back on heading and on your planned altitude before going any further. Get an initial heading either by making a sensible guess, or by using a ruler against the nearest VOR rose. Write the new heading down and then fly the aircraft on that new heading and altitude. Apply the drift to the track that you calculated on the ground using your windstar (more on that later), or by making a sensible educated guess. Practice making sensible heading guesses as you fly, as you will surprised how accurate you can be without

Navigation

having to use a protractor. However, do go back and check the heading when you can, to be sure you have got it right as it is easy to make mistakes when under pressure.

Write the track and the heading down and then fly the aircraft by returning to check your heading and altitude. Remember you are still expected to fly the aircraft within limits while doing the planning, so it is so important to keep looking up and out, at your instruments as well as at the horizon. If you haven't done a windstar or you want a different way, then make a sensible guess as to the drift by halving the forecast wind as the maximum drift and then imagine a 90-degree angle. Divide the angle into 30-degree sections and use a third of the maximum drift at the 30-degree angle, two thirds at the 60-degree angle and the rest at full maximum drift.

The windstar is a really useful way of getting an accurate drift and groundspeed for the various points of a compass so you don't have to calculate them in the air. You won't know where you will be diverted to or when, so make sure you fill in the drift and groundspeed for eight points of the compass and then, no

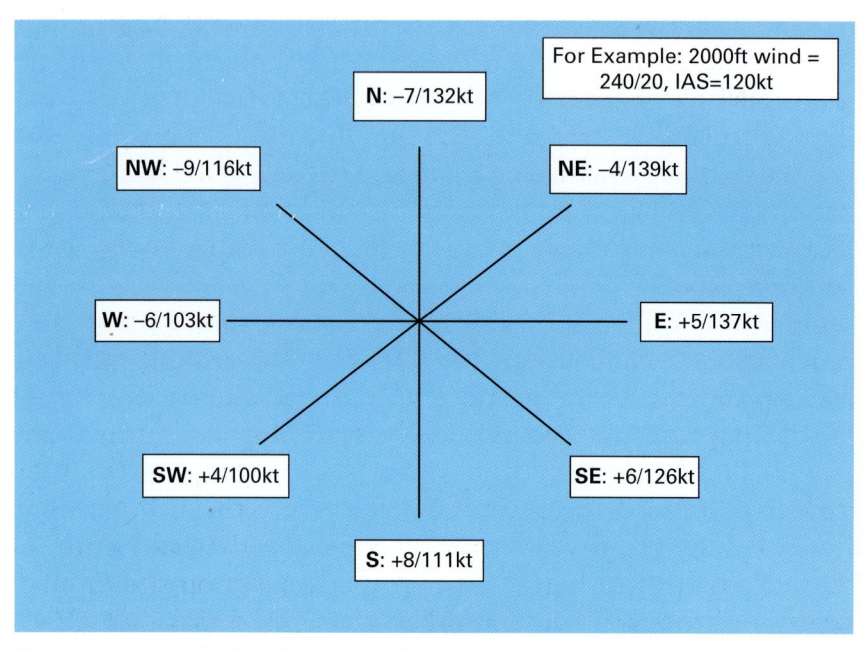

For Example: 2000ft wind = 240/20, IAS=120kt

N: −7/132kt
NW: −9/116kt
NE: −4/139kt
W: −6/103kt
E: +5/137kt
SW: +4/100kt
SE: +6/126kt
S: +8/111kt

The windstar – useful for instrument flying as well as navigation.

matter where you are sent on your diversion, you have that information to hand on your plog or chart. Obviously you will need to use your CRP and write down the drift and groundspeed at the points of the compass using the forecast wind you planned the navigation with before you take-off.

The spot winds can be found on the Form 214 from the Met Office website – make sure you are using the nearest and most accurate wind strength, and monitor the temperature forecast at that altitude in case of icing. Also, by preparing the windstar before you go also means that you have an accurate drift in degrees for your instrument flying – VOR and NDB tracking – because you can apply the drift to the heading you are going to steer from the windstar for accurate tracking from the beginning.

You may have to plan a diversion around a gliding site or danger area for example, as well as the official diversion. One example of planning a diversion around an obstacle is:

1. Divert 60 degrees to the left or right of track for a fixed period of time, e.g. 2 minutes, depending on whether you have a headwind or tailwind (obviously make a note of how long you use).
2. Parallel your original track for the same time.
3. Turn back by 60 degrees for the same time.
4. Take up your original heading and hopefully track.

Don't forget to advise ATC of what you are doing, or else if you are being followed on radar they will ask, which could mean an unnecessary interruption just when you are busy planning.

If you lose your ruler, remember your thumb is about 10nm long (on a 1:500,000 chart). Get a ruler out (make sure no one is watching) and check if you don't believe me.

Remember to draw a halfway point on your map and complete the Time–Turn–Talk–Gross Error–FREDA checks as they will bring up any off-track or timing issues. You won't have a drift line so you will need to make a sensible guess of the number of degrees off track you are – *if* you are – and apply the appropriate correction.

Navigation

Lastly, try to give some thought to the following as they could cause you some issues on your diversion leg. I have called them DRAAG checks as it is easy to remember:

D – Danger areas
R – Restricted areas
A – Airspace
A – Airfields
G – Glider sites (and ballooning sites)

If you find you have any of the above on your diversion leg, be sure to point them out and your intention of how you are going to deal with them. For example, mention the height of the danger or restricted area and whether you are to fly over safely or whether you will have to plan a diversion around it.

Study the map (do it in your spare time as well, especially if you haven't flown in UK airspace before), study the ground features carefully and keep an open mind that you could be anywhere (though you shouldn't be that disorientated if you follow these procedures). Make sure you log all changes in heading, altitude and times on your plog as neatly as you can so you can follow your calculations if you have to go back over them. (It's a good habit to get into now as it is very important on the IR that the flight can be recreated by what you have written down.)

As I explained, you are allowed to use any available navigation aids on your diversion. I would recommend you use a VOR/DME for a position fix if you want to confirm your position, or else as a backup to confirm when you are overhead your diversion point. You must of course identify any radio aid – note that it is a fail if you use one without identifying it. I know – it nearly cost me my CPL skill test.

Unless you are fluent in Morse code (which most pilots these days are not!), it is a good idea is to write down the Morse ident for each and every VOR in area so there can be no mistake as to which VOR/DME you are using. Also write down the Morse ident for the letters 'TST' as this is what you will hear if the VOR/DME is unserviceable. It should be NOTAM'd if navigation aids are unserviceable (which you will have read hopefully!) but you need to be prepared. Also, make a mark in permanent marker on any VORs you may use on each of the 10-degree lines, especially if the VOR rose on the map is obscured by other features on the map. It will make it easier and more accurate for you to read off the radial for the position fix.

And finally ... as you approach about 2nm to your diversion point, give your instructor or the examiner three reasons why you are where you say you are. If you have used a VOR/DME for a position fix over the diversion point, you can also point that out. Once you are overhead, but you lose sight of the diversion point, you may orbit. Be confident and positive and you should be where you need to be.

GETTING A POSITION FIX

Find the nearest VOR/DME on your chart, tune in the frequency, listen to the ident and then turn the OBS knob until the needle is centred with a 'from' flag. Read off the radial from the head of the needle and draw a line from the centre of the VOR out to at least 15cm on your chart. Then tune and identify the DME frequency. Note that if it is slaved to Nav 1 you must make sure it is selected to Nav 1, if that is the one you are using. Many students have got the position fix hopelessly wrong by putting the frequency into Nav 1 but tuning to Nav 2 VOR and using that for the position fix. I have also seen them do it with the DME: identing Nav 1 but with Nav 2 selected as the DME setting. Don't get caught out like that.

Read off the distance on the DME and make a mark on the chart to show the examiner where you are. Mark a circle and allow for the fact the aircraft is still travelling at 120kt (note that this is the Piper Arrow speed and may be different from the aircraft type you are flying); the needle may not be centred anymore if you are not flying in the same direction. Re-centre the needle and re-draw the line if you have to, as the fix needs to be accurate.

The other way of using the position fix is if you want to confirm your position overhead your diversion point, you should draw a line from the centre of the VOR/DME to the diversion point. Once you are overhead, in theory the CDI needle should be in the centre. Don't forget to tune and identify the VOR/DME. Read off the radial that the line passes over your diversion

Navigation

on your chart, and set the CDI up to show that radial. Make a note of the DME distance and again, in theory, once the CDI is centred and the DME is showing the same number of miles as you expect, you should be overhead.

Remember you can orbit if you can't see the diversion point, but be aware of your speed and altitude in the turn – entering a steep descending dive and losing hundreds of feet while looking for your diversion point is not only a fail point, but very easy to do and obviously very dangerous, so keep looking out.

So, ideally, you will then reach your diversion point, within plus or minus three minutes of the ETA you gave the examiner with three ground features that confirm you are where you think you are, and hopefully without busting any controlled airspace. If so, then congratulations, you have passed your navigation section!

If the navigation is not working out as expected, don't panic or, even worse, give up. If things are going wrong, you need to triple your concentration and efforts to get yourself to your destination. Turn any irritation or annoyance with yourself into adrenaline to get the job done – get annoyed with yourself on the ground as it is cheaper and won't impact on the rest of the skill test. Don't let a small worry turn into a complete fail. Also, don't assume you are where you think you are or where your finger is on the map. So many of us keep our finger on the map where we think we are without allowing for the fact that the aircraft is moving along. Therefore, you should move your finger along the map at 120kt or whatever the cruise speed is of your aircraft.

8 Emergencies

The propeller is just a big fan in the front of the plane to keep the pilot cool. Want proof? Make it stop, then watch the pilot break out in a sweat.

Anon.

There are three main types of emergency situation in the air that you must learn for the skill test: engine fire in the air, catastrophic engine failure in the air, and a rough-running engine in the air. In addition, you must learn the drill for engine failure after take-off (EFATO). There is always a simulated EFATO after each emergency.

However, be aware that the examiner could ask you about any kind of emergency while in the air or on the ground – such as engine fire on start-up or an electrical fire in the air – so read the aircraft POH and checklists, and be familiar with them. If you are at all unsure of the drill procedure for any emergency situation the examiner gives you, the correct response to them is 'I will get the checklist out.' This is the response that will prepare you for the airline's Standard Operating Procedures (SOPs) as well as the Quick Reference Handbooks (QRHs).

> **These drills are 'touch drills' only, unless it happens for real!**

You will notice that there is repetition in some of the description of procedures that occur during the drills, but this is for completeness and reduces any confusion, so bear with it. And be aware that there are quite a few potential failure points in this section, so make sure you know the drills perfectly. These drills are written as they are taught, but if your ATO does things differently, then obviously you should do what they teach you.

ENGINE FIRE IN THE AIR

The examiner will indicate that you have a (simulated) engine fire in the air by saying something along the lines of 'You have smoke and fire coming out the engine.'

Make sure you understand what the examiner is asking you to do, as you will fail the section if you perform a perfect engine fire drill, but he really asked you for a catastrophic engine failure drill or a rough-running engine. Remember again that these are touch drills unless specified otherwise.

You will need to perform the checks as detailed in your training organization's checklist as soon as you have been told the nature of the drill, then ask the examiner if the fire is out and if the propeller has stopped. If the answer is 'Yes, the propeller has stopped but the fire is not out', you will need to enter the emergency descent. If the answer is 'No, the propeller hasn't stopped and the fire is not out', you will need to pitch up a few degrees to simulate slowing the propeller down and then ask the question again. You should then get a reply that the propeller has stopped but the fire is not out – hence the need for the emergency descent!

To enter the emergency descent, smoothly close the throttle, pitch the nose up to get the speed into the white arc, promptly put all three stages of flap on and then pitch the aircraft nose down for 100kt.

During the descent, get the (simulated) MAYDAY call done as soon as possible and simulate setting 7700 on the transponder. Keep the MAYDAY call short and sweet, so say something along the lines of 'Station name, callsign, MAYDAY MAYDAY MAYDAY, engine fire, three on board, position, forced landing in a field.' Be sure to review the official MAYDAY call. The reason to get them done in the descent is to save you time later on in the drill when all your attention is focussed on a safe landing.

Once you have got 95–100kt on the ASI and you have completed the MAYDAY call and transponder setting, ask the examiner if the fire is out. If they reply 'Yes, the fire is out', pitch the nose smoothly up out of the descent, be sure the speed is in the white arc and get the aircraft clean (bring all stages of flap up as soon as possible) while pitching up and then down towards the best glide speed. Then start to turn into wind to look for a field.

Use the altimeter to decide how far away to look for a field: if you are at 1,000ft, the field needs to be closer than if you are at 2,000ft. However, never look further away than the 180-degree arc from wing tip to wing tip as a Piper Arrow with the landing gear down and three stages of flap down has all the gliding characteristics of a concrete bollard.

It is highly unlikely that the examiner will say 'No, the fire is not out', but if he does, then you must continue the drill and get the aircraft on the ground as soon as possible.

Despite what it says in some training books, there is not usually a convenient smoke stack showing you where the wind is coming from, and in the heat of the moment of doing the drill it is very easy to forget to turn into wind. So, if in doubt, turn onto the runway heading that you took off from, as you should only ever have a crosswind component for landing, rather than a tailwind component. If you can remember which way the wind sock was pointing while you did your captain's brief back at the hold so much the better, as you can simply point the aircraft to the left or right of the runway heading, as required.

It is normally a fail point if you try to land with any form of tailwind component unless you have chosen a field so large that it would not affect the safety of the landing. There are few such fields in most of the UK, so it is best that you always assume that a tailwind component is a fail point.

Once you have selected a field (ideally into wind), then you need to start immediately on a passenger brief while maintaining the best glide speed. There is no need to repeat what you said in the

> *Try to remember the five 'S's when choosing a field: Shape, Surface, Size, Surround and Slope.*

main passenger brief, so just say something along the lines of 'Ladies and Gentleman, we appear to have an in-flight emergency. Please take up the brace position on my command.' Keep assessing the distance to the field you have chosen. Ideally, you shouldn't need to change the field you have chosen because you

Emergencies

are too high or too low. If you *are* too high, you have a few options such as extending the landing gear (put it down when you will definitely make your chosen field), or 'S' turns or positioning by turning away and then back. However, if you are too low or obstacles appear in the field, you will have to choose an alternate field. That is why it is good to pick a field in a large open area with lots of other fields around it. You must make sure you do an engine warm during this practice emergency descent, so open and close the throttle for 3 seconds every 1,000ft you lose in the descent.

A major fail point that often seems come up is aiming to touchdown in the centre or even two thirds of the way down the field even with the landing gear and flaps down. Believe me, it isn't what the examiner wants. It is tempting to stay high until the last second, but part of the exercise is that you are demonstrating you know the gliding ability of the aircraft and the examiner wants you aiming to touchdown just after the threshold of the field you have chosen. The examiner would rather you made it to the threshold with one stage of flap on than have all three stages down but under-shoot.

However, assuming that you have completed your drills, and it is all looking good for a safe touchdown, the last simulated call you need to make out loud is 'Master switch off, door latched, Brace, Brace, Brace.' (Door latched or unlatched? Check your aircraft's POH.)

The examiner will at some stage call for a go-around. Do not try to pre-empt his call by having your hand hovering over the throttle. The correct go-around procedure is:

1. Full power
2. Positive pitch up
3. Raise the drag flap (flap 3)
4. Positive rate of climb
5. Landing gear up
6. Positive rate of climb
7. Raise the second stage of flap up
8. Positive rate of climb
9. Raise the first stage of flap up

> **Top Tip**
>
> Don't climb away over a large village or town; you don't want to find yourself with a real engine failure and unable to glide clear.

10. Set the correct climb power setting
11. Climb away at the best rate of climb speed
12. Do a clearing weave and then one every 1,000ft until you level off in the cruise

And one last note on the engine fire drill: as a variation on a theme of the engine fire, the examiner could tell you that you have an engine fire with smoke and flames coming out of the left- or right-hand side of the engine. The only change in the drill is that in the emergency descent you will need to apply rudder to the side that the smoke is coming out of. Just be aware that this will rapidly increase your rate of descent so you may have less altitude and therefore time in which to get the rest of the drills done. The way to remember which rudder to use is 'stamp on the fire.'

CATASTROPHIC ENGINE FAILURE IN THE AIR

This varies from the engine fire in the air as the examiner will indicate that you have a (simulated) catastrophic engine failure in the air by saying something along the lines of 'The engine has gone bang and you have oil all over the windscreen.'

Make sure you understand exactly what type of emergency you are being asked to demonstrate.

You will need to perform the checks as detailed in your training organization's checklist as soon as you have been told of the drill. As there is (in theory) no way that you will get any further power from the engine, the priority is to get the best glide speed. So physically close the throttle, pitch up for the best glide speed

Emergencies

and turn into wind while looking for a suitable field to land in. Once you have selected it, then you need to shut down the engine as per your training course notes.

During the descent, get the MAYDAY call done quickly and simulate setting 7700 on the transponder. Keep the MAYDAY call brief, along the lines of 'Station name, callsign, MAYDAY MAYDAY MAYDAY, engine failure, three on board, position, forced landing in a field.' Review the MAYDAY call if required.

As for the emergency fire drill, use the altimeter to decide how far away to look for a field: the lower you are, the closer the field needs to be. However, never look further away than the 180-degree arc from wing tip to wing tip.

Make sure you do not land with a tailwind component, as this will almost certainly be a fail point. If in doubt, turn onto the runway heading that you took off from, if possible pointing the aircraft to the left or right of the runway heading as suggested by the windsock direction relative to the runway when you took off.

Once you have selected a field (ideally into wind) and performed the shut-down checks as per your checklist, you need to start immediately on a passenger brief while maintaining the best glide speed. There is no need to repeat what you said in the main passenger brief, so just say something along the lines of 'Ladies and Gentleman, we appear to have an in-flight emergency. Please take up the brace position on my command.' Keep assessing the distance to the field you have chosen, getting rid of excess height by extending the landing gear, making 'S' turns or positioning by turning away.

If you are too low or obstacles appear in the field, you will have to choose an alternate field. You must make sure you keep the engine warm during this descent.

However, assuming that you have completed your drills, and it is all looking good for a safe touchdown, the last simulated call you need to make out loud is 'Master switch off, door latched,

---

Top Tip

Check your POH as to whether the door should be latched closed or left open for an emergency landing.

Brace, Brace, Brace'. The examiner will at some stage call for a go-around, but do not try to pre-empt his call by having your hand hovering over the throttle.

RE-STARTABLE ENGINE FAILURE IN THE AIR

The examiner will indicate that you have a (simulated) re-startable engine failure in the air by saying something along the lines of 'The engine is rough running.' As already mentioned, make sure you know what the examiner is asking you to do as you will fail the section if he asks you for a re-startable engine fire drill but you perform a catastrophic engine failure drill.

You will need to perform the checks as detailed in your training organization's checklist as soon as

> *Remember: These drills are 'touch drills' only unless it happens for real.*

you have been told of the appropriate emergency. As there is a chance that you will not get any more power from the engine, the priority is to get the best glide speed. Close the throttle, pitch up for the best glide speed and turn into wind while looking for a suitable field to land in. Once you have selected it, then you need to try to restart the engine as per your training course notes.

Now ask the examiner if the engine has restarted. If 'no', then continue with the descent into your field, get the MAYDAY call done and simulate setting 7700 on the transponder. Use the altimeter to decide how far away to look for a field, and never look further away than the 180-degree arc from wing tip to wing tip. Avoid at all costs landing with a tailwheel component, if necessary using the same heading for landing as the runway you took off from, if possible adjusting left or right in line with the position of the windsock when you took off.

Once you have selected a field and performed the shut down checks, perform a passenger brief while maintaining the best glide speed. Keep assessing the distance to the field you have chosen, remembering options for losing excess height such as extending the landing gear, 'S' turns and positioning by turning away. Keep the engine warm during this descent.

Emergencies

Avoid the temptation to stay high until the last second, and aim to touch down just after the threshold of the field you have chosen. Having completed your drills, if it is all looking good for a safe touchdown, the last simulated call you need to make out loud is 'Master switch off, door latched, Brace, Brace, Brace.' The examiner will at some stage call for a go-around, but do not try to pre-empt his call by having your hand hovering over the throttle.

There are two variations on a theme for the re-startable engine failure. You could be told that there is a strange knocking noise coming from somewhere on the aircraft. What the examiner is looking for is for you to check the engine temperatures and pressures before you do anything else. This is to establish whether it is actually the engine that is making the noise, or whether it could be that you have shut the cabin door with the end of the harness hanging out, and the harness is banging vigorously against the fuselage. I have had this happen and it makes a worryingly loud noise.

You could also be told that the oil temperature gauge is showing a high temperature along with a low oil pressure reading. What the examiner is looking for is for you to check the engine temperatures and pressures before you do anything else like shutting the engine down. The engine is still running reasonably happily at this stage, so the examiner is looking for you to monitor the gauges while planning an immediate diversion to the nearest airfield. If the examiner then tells you the engine has now started rough running, you would start the engine rough running drill.

ENGINE FAILURE AFTER TAKE-OFF (EFATO)

Immediately after the go-around and the aircraft has been cleaned up – i.e. gear and flaps up and in the climb – the examiner will close the throttle and declare an engine failure after take-off. Your immediate reaction must be to pitch the nose down into the glide descent attitude (e.g. 80kt glide), then select a field within 30 degrees of either side of the nose and then, once you will make the threshold of the chosen field, select the gear down, call 'BRACE, BRACE, BRACE' and master switch off. Whether you will have time to do any further checks or a MAYDAY call depends on your altitude when the throttle is closed, but the priority obviously is to fly the aircraft and land safely.

Examples of other emergencies you may be asked are: brake failure on the ground, smoke in the cabin and electrical fire in the air, but these can all be responded to by getting the checklist out and reading it out. However, I would recommend you read the checklist and POH, and be familiar with them before your test.

Finally, remember to do FREDA checks every 15 minutes during the lesson and change the fuel tanks every 30 minutes. The examiner will normally take responsibility for the radio during this section, but you must still be responsible for the lookout.

If you are ever faced with a forced landing at night, turn on the landing light to see the landing area. If you don't like what you see, turn 'em back off.

Anon.

9 170A AND CPL SKILL TEST

Truly superior pilots are those who use their superior judgement to avoid those situations where they might have to use their superior skill.

Anon.

You will only be put up for a 170A and the skill test when you are ready and can fly within the skill test parameters, so even if you don't quite believe it yourself, have faith in the fact that your instructor believes you can do it. Do have a look at the CPL Skill Test Standards Document, either on the CAA website for the full syllabus or at the end of this chapter for the exact details of the skill test tolerances.

There is also a guide in the Appendix to the weather minima you should look at for your 170A and skill test, which will help you make a sensible decision on whether you should fly the test on a particular day. Don't forget that it is your decision to fly or not to fly – but also consider any advice offered.

THE 170A

The 170A is the pre-test test. (It is named after the form that is filled in by the examiner that shows that your flying is up to test standard.) The 170A flight test is not a CAA requirement of the course, but many schools expect you to fly a full skill test with an in-house examiner as a way of determining whether you are ready for the real skill test. You will be expected to fly it as if it is a real test, and the examiner will be particularly hard on you and all aspects of your flying. Trust me when I say that the 170A will make the skill test seem very easy! It may even seem in the debrief as if you did nothing right, but remember that the examiner is being critical for your own benefit. Try to make notes in the debrief of everything the examiner tells you, as it is unlikely you will remember what they said just a few minutes later. The pressure of probably a lack of sleep from the night before, being up early to pre-flight and plan, and the stress of the flight usually lead to amnesia! But they are points that you will need to take on board, so do listen.

It is not unusual for the 170A examiner to suggest or recommend some revision flying training before you are submitted for test, as most pilots will make some kind of mistake on their 170A. If you fail one section, it is normally recommended to have a lesson with your instructor on whatever you failed on, but if it is a full fail because you have failed two sections out of the five, you may well have to do more revision training and another 170A test, which can really rack up the hours. Helping you to avoid those expensive re-training flights is of course one of the objectives of this book.

The brief for the 170A and skill test is pretty much the same. Therefore, though the next section refers to the skill test, it stands for the 170A as well.

THE SKILL TEST

The CPL skill test will be arranged by the flying school once you have successfully completed the 170A (and not before, no matter how hard you pester your instructor!). Normally, an external CAA CPL examiner will be brought in (this can be arranged within a couple of days). You will need to call the CAA at Gatwick to pay the test fee prior to the test – the phone number can be found on the CAA website or at the back of this book. They will need to know the date of your test, your PPL licence number and your credit or debit card details. They will then fax confirmation that the fee has been paid, and this receipt needs to be given to the examiner, who may refuse to test you if you don't have it.

Each time you take a CPL skill test, it is called an 'attempt', and these are grouped into 'series'. There are two attempts in each series. There is no limit to the number of series that may be taken. If you partially fail on your first attempt, you will be asked to retake the departure and the section that was failed. The first retake is called the second attempt in the first series.

170A and CPL Skill Test

A full fail means your retest is a first attempt in the second series. A free retest may be awarded if the test is stopped with the agreement of you (the student) and the examiner, and only for those sections not flown. If the student stops the test with the examiner *not* in agreement, then you may forfeit the test and fee. The 170A covers two attempts. If you don't test within six months of the date of the 170A, it becomes invalid and you will need to pass another one – so probably best to get it right, or as close to right as you can the first time!

BEFORE TEST DAY

Your instructor will know who your examiner is a few days before the real test and will arrange for you to get contact details for him. This is because you will need to contact them the night before the test to introduce yourself, discuss the weather and the suitability of the weather for the test and ask his weight (politely!) so you can do the mass and balance calculations. The examiner may also give you a navigation route to plan if you are testing first thing in the morning (possibly even two routes, if the weather is not looking great).

Do make sure you can do the mass and balance and maybe even the performance calculations for your particular aircraft happily and successfully, well before the night before the test. You do not want to be unsure of how to do them and be struggling with them alone with no access to a friendly and helpful instructor while worrying about the test the next day! Also, calculate the calm wind conditions as well as the forecast wind for all the runways at your home airfield in case you can't land on the runway you took off from. It may seem like a lot of work, but you don't want to find yourself unsure as to whether a change of runway could cause you to go-around and or divert to another airfield.

However, be aware that the examiner could give you your navigation route during the initial brief on the morning of the test and give you time to plan it afterwards. In this case there is not much you can plan the night before, so get yourself a checklist of all the things you need to take with you in the morning so you don't have a mad scramble to get yourself together in the morning, when you are likely to forget something.

Make sure your logbook and your student records agree as far as flight times and lessons flown go, as well making sure you have met the minimum hours for the IF. Do this on a bad weather day with your instructor over a cup of coffee, not at the last minute. Also, get a print-out of your hours flown from your ATO and check it for any mistakes or discrepancies – you may even by due a refund!

A word about money. The whole test could take up to two and a half hours, but is usually just under two hours. This may not have been quoted in your initial quote for the CPL course, so be aware of this hidden cost. You will also have to pay any approach fees and the test fee. (To pay for your skill test means a phone call to the CAA at Gatwick. Make sure you have your PPL licence number and credit card to hand, and the date and place of your test.)

TEST DAY

The examiner will arrange a time to meet up with you for the initial briefing. If the weather is forecast to be totally unsuitable (and remember that it is your command decision as to whether to go) then a new test date and time will be arranged for you – and you won't lose your test fee. If however, the weather forecast is 50/50 as to whether it will go ahead, then you will need to call the examiner first thing in the morning to confirm the plan.

All the CAA examiners are very experienced pilots, with years of instructing and examining, and all of them are truly lovely people. They all remember what it is like to fly a skill test, and there is absolutely no need to be scared of them. The only reason you could lose your test fee is if you elect not to fly and the weather is more than good enough, but that very rarely happens as the decision not to go is usually done together. The examiner will do their best to put you at your ease and make the test as enjoyable and smooth as possible.

You will need to arrive at least thirty minutes before the meeting time, suitably attired in black trousers and white shirt and black tie (girls and guys!). It isn't compulsory to get dressed up, but this marks the start of your professional career and gives a good impression to the examiner. You will need to make sure you have with you and/or available in the aircraft:

- a valid medical
- valid PPL and SEP
- valid RT licence and English proficiency certificate
- completed plog including fuel calculations
- completed mass/balance and performance calculations for actual and calm wind conditions
- a spare headset
- current NOTAMS, TAF, METAR and spot winds with all the relevant information highlighted
- two aircraft checklists
- suitable and approved screens for the IF as well as a cover for the AI and DI for simulating limited panel
- aircraft documents including C of A, insurance, tech log, Aeroplane Approval Certificate (F176) and the ARC
- up to date and complete logbook
- receipt confirming payment of skill test
- a valid form of identity: valid passport, UK Forces ID, airport pass
- any relevant CAA correspondence if required
- Up to date chart
- Completed windstar and rules, pens etc as required

Try to get the aircraft you are testing in refuelled the previous night (unless it is flying before your test), as it will be one less thing for you to worry about on the morning of your test. Also, make sure the screens for the instrument flying are available and fit correctly if you are using them. Make sure you arrive in plenty of time for the brief to allow for traffic – even consider staying on site if possible so as to avoid any worries about traffic etc.

If there are more than one of you testing that day and you are not testing first, the examiner will give you your route just before leaving on the first test, so you will have about two hours to plan without any external help from fellow students or instructors.

Your flight log must show route, communication and navigation frequencies, planned levels or altitudes, timings, ETA, MSA, safety altitude/height or minimum levels/altitudes, fuel including contingency, fuel remaining, room for logging ATIS and clearances in chronological order. You are not allowed to use pre-planned routes but electronic planning devices are allowed. If using the latter be careful, as nerves could cause finger trouble and some peculiar headings may ensue. Do what is called a sanity check – that the headings, times and the rest all look sensible and you haven't made silly mistakes.

Lastly, your aircraft performance must be calculated for the most limiting of runways and wind: calm, as well as the current weather conditions for the TORA, TODA and LDA.

The Brief

In the brief, the examiner will go through the paperwork as detailed above, and will then ask some questions about the aircraft and the nominated speeds at which you will fly. Make sure you know the cruise, glide, flapless and Vref. The examiner will then explain the nature of the flight: you are flying a professional, commercial, passenger-paying flight, and they want the route flown as such.

They will expect you to treat them as an interested passenger, so you need to keep a running commentary of what you are doing in flight; then they will know what you are doing and why, and they hopefully won't have to ask you too many questions. This also means giving the passenger brief, making sure they are comfortable in flight and generally happy. They will also ask you about what privileges having a CPL gives you, so make sure you read the most up-to-date information available. For example, as a CPL holder can you fly an aerial photographic flight at night or over water?

Applicants are potentially tested on all of the CPL skill test syllabus and also airmanship, RT, basic handing skill and general management of the flight in a professional manner and to the standards set by EASA and the CAA. Keep in mind that passenger safety, comfort and reassurance are also an important part of how you conduct the flight.

170A and CPL Skill Test

> **Top Tip**
>
> Try not to get so nervous on test day that you come across as excessively stressed and wound up. The examiners are well aware that this is a tough time and will give allowances for nerves and try to put you at ease, but try not to give the impression of being completely terrified by them. Examiners have feelings, too!

The examiner will then explain the content of the test which usually goes along the lines of:

- Departure
- En-route navigation and diversion
- IF
- Circuits
- General airwork and emergencies
- Arrival

Obviously this may change depending on the weather, the practicality of doing circuits at your home or other airfield, and so on. The examiner will explain that a failure in one section will result in a partial pass and a failure in two sections will warrant a full fail. If this happens, the examiner will take control of the aircraft and stop the test and return to your base airfield.

During the Test Flight
The exact order of the test is at the examiner's discretion, and be aware you may also be verbally questioned on such things as aircraft performance, technical aspects of the aircraft and the like. All the sections of the test are to be completed in the course of one flight.

Note that any ATC instructions must be followed, even if they conflict with the examiner's brief. The examiner will ask for the speeds you will fly, which you are expected to adhere to. If you need to change them because of a change of flying conditions, you will need to advise the examiner of your new

170A and CPL Skill Test

target speed. (If you don't tell them about any changes, then they will start to think that you can't fly to CPL standards so keep them informed with a short explanation.)

Try to treat each section as an individual test, so once one section is over, delete it from your mind (the good bits and the bad bits) and mentally move on to the next part of the test.

What you think is a catastrophic and an appalling bit of flying in a section may well have been missed or overlooked by the examiner – they could have been looking out the window at the time. So don't deliberately point out any of your heading or altitude errors. Even if you do make a mistake, correct it as soon as you see it, and don't forget that the examiner will make certain allowances for nerves, turbulence and so on, and they are allowed to ask you to repeat certain manoeuvres. So don't despair and don't dwell on any mistakes, real or perceived, as you will certainly end up focussing on something that is not important (or something that you can't now change) to the detriment of the rest of the skill test. That doesn't mean the examiner will excuse sloppy flying or poor airmanship, but unless you are told otherwise on the ground or in the air, you have passed – so believe in yourself.

If there is a real in-flight emergency, you will be expected to deal with it as per your training and the checklists, but the examiner may elect to take control at any stage.

> **Don't forget those FREDA checks!**

Top Tip

Treat the examiner as an interested passenger and try not to 'do' anymore than you have been taught in an attempt to impress, usually backfires. Just fly as you have been taught, keep busy and keep ahead of the aircraft.

After the Test
Once the test is over, you will not necessarily be told immediately whether you have passed or not, so don't assume the

worst. In the debrief, accept the result with good humour (whether a pass, fail or partial) and don't argue over the points that are brought up. Just because you don't remember doing it, doesn't mean that you didn't do it. If you can, make notes in the debrief, especially if you need them for a re-test. You can only challenge the conduct of a test, not the outcome, and that must be done within fourteen days of test.

If you have passed first time, congratulations! If you have partialled (i.e. failed only one section), then congratulations too. You will be told if you need any compulsory training before your re-test. If you have failed because you failed two out of the five sections, then commiserations. However, don't despair: you will no doubt be thoroughly annoyed, but remember that this is all useful flying training experience and those hours all count. Lastly, try to maintain a professional demeanour from the moment you meet the examiner to the time the debrief is over, even if the result is not what you expected or hoped for.

CPL SKILL TEST TOLERANCES

Listed below are the official skill test tolerances that you will need to adhere to unless you have a very good reason not to. However, these tolerances should not be achieved at the expense of a smooth and co-ordinated flight! They have been taken from the Flight Examiners Handbook and the CPL Standards documents.

Altitude
  Cruise: +/−100ft
  Simulated engine failure: +/−150ft
  Limited or partial panel: +/−200ft

Tracking
  All approaches except precision: +/−5 degrees

Heading
  All engine operating: +/−10 degrees
  Simulated engine failure: +/−15 degrees
  Limited or partial panel: +/−15 degrees

Speed
  Take-off: +5kt/−0kt
  Climb: +/−10kt
  Vat/Vref: +5kt/−0kt
  Cruise: +/−10kt
  Limited or partial panel: +/−10kt
  Simulated engine failure: +10kt/−5kt
  Max airspeed error at any time: +/−10kt

TYPICAL TEST QUESTIONS

Answer to the earlier question: not a legal flight as a CPL in a single-engine aircraft – you will have to bolt another engine onto the wing!

Other useful questions you should know the answers to for your aircraft type are:

1. What are the hot start and flooded start engine techniques?
2. What is the rated horsepower?
3. How long will the battery support the electrics in the event of an emergency?
4. What is the voltage of the electrical system and battery?
5. What prevents the landing gear being retracted on the ground?
6. What would you do if you did not see the gear down and locked indications?
7. Is the stall warning horn an electrical or mechanical design?
8. If installed, how is the auto-pilot disabled or over-powered?
9. What is the MTOW of the aeroplane?
10. What is the maximum weight that can be carried in the baggage compartment?
11. What is the maximum airspeed to be used during flight in rough air when lightly loaded?
12. What speed would you use on short final for a short field landing?

10 Common Student Mistakes and Failure Points

Rule one: no matter what else happens, fly the aircraft.

Anon.

The advice given in this chapter derives from not only years of instructing but also from listening to literally hundreds of skill test and 170A debriefs. These points have been brought up by the examiners, some of them over and over and over again. If you do nothing with this book but read and learn from this chapter, you will still get a head start on most other CPL student pilots.

As a general rule, a good lookout should be the easiest thing to do but seems to be the hardest part of the course for some. The examiners can and will fail you for a poor lookout even if you fly a perfect skill test, and invariably the lookout is something that has deteriorated since your PPL. A good lookout before each manoeuvre is not only needed but crucial for a first-time pass. Make large, big movements of your head and eyes, scanning from wing tip to wing tip as well as up and down. It's the same principle that you were taught in your driving lessons: mirror, signal, manoeuvre.

SECTION 1 – CIRCUITS

Common mistakes:

- Being 'behind the aircraft': i.e. being slow with checks, radio calls and so on

Common Student Mistakes and Failure Points

- Sitting on errors: coming off heading or altitude but making little or no effort to get the aircraft back to the correct heading or altitude
- If you aren't doing something, you have forgotten something: you should always be busy even if only doing a FREDA check or looking out for other traffic
- Lookout all around and through all the windows, not just looking out a small part of the windscreen in front of you. You need to be moving your head and looking out from wing tip to wing tip, and up and down, every few seconds
- Poor join: slow to request joining instructions, slow to descend, slow to get pre-landing checks done, not seeing airfield early enough, not getting the ATIS
- Taking too much power off to descend in time so the gear warning horn goes off and exceeding 750fpm
- Not setting up the CDI to runway orientation and using it for cross-wind, downwind and base headings as part of the airfield approach checks
- Configuring for base without the pre-landing checks having been completed.

Fail points:

- Not joining as cleared to, such as being told left base and actually joining downwind
- Not knowing which is the dead side/live side of the circuit
- Positioning for the wrong runway
- Not allowing for drift in the circuit pattern
- Not making it to the threshold on the glide approach, or trying to extend the glide with a low airspeed
- Not using or responding quickly enough to the PAPIs to get on the correct glideslope
- Not landing abeam the runway numbers or the PAPIs if asked to
- Touching down on a displaced threshold
- Not identifying radio aids.

SECTION 2 – GENERAL AIRWORK

Common mistakes:

- Poor RT: sloppy Basic Service call, not getting all the information over in one transmission, missing calls by talking over transmissions
- Not pulling the control column back while taxying on grass and not having a good lookout before doing the power checks
- Taxying too quickly, i.e. faster than a walking speed
- Rushing or failing to do checks in the correct order on the checklist
- Not reporting your position in circuit or when requested to
- Not maintaining heading or altitude between manoeuvres
- Not using rudder in take-off roll and in the climb to balance the aircraft
- No clearing weave in climb, especially climbing out after an EFATO.

Fail points:

- Taking too long for a position fix or an inaccurate fix
- Excessive height loss or gain in the stall entry and recovery
- Getting the stall entry and recovery in the wrong order
- Losing a positive rate of climb in the stall recovery
- Not allowing for wind strength in PFL
- Lining up to take off with an aircraft on final
- Not hearing or responding to an 'all traffic' QNH change.

SECTION 3 – INSTRUMENT FLYING

Common mistakes:

- Not getting settled quickly or taking too long to start the manoeuvres
- Not asking if you are cleared to turn
- Not bugging your new heading before turning.

Fail points:

- Not knowing or giving the wrong MSA
- Not initiating the IF checks while in cloud or simulated cloud conditions
- Excessive height loss or gain in the manoeuvres
- Incorrect order of recovery in limited panel unusual attitude recovery
- Taking more than two attempts at the limited panel compass turns to get onto heading
- Becoming disorientated under screens and not responding to the instruments correctly
- Incorrect AOB used in turns.

SECTION 4 – NAVIGATION

Common mistakes:

- Not identifying navigation aids or wrongly identifying them when using them
- Not setting the correct QNH at the start of the navigation leg
- Not mentioning regional QNH change if flying on a local QNH, i.e. crossing into new ASR
- Not correcting heading or track or altitude errors in good time.

Fail points:

- Flying past the destination or diversion without mentioning them
- Not knowing where you are or giving wrong position reports
- Misidentifying features or towns
- Not speaking to an ATZ if flying within 5nm of it
- Not requesting zone transit if flying over an ATZ
- Entering controlled airspace without permission
- Not setting a QNH when given
- Not setting the regional QNH, e.g. if on London Info or Farnborough LARS.

SECTION 5 – EMERGENCIES

Common mistakes:

- No or incomplete passenger brief
- Picking a field too far away to glide to, or getting too high and too close
- Poor lookout in descent
- No clearing weave on climb out from EFATO
- Taking too long with mayday call and 7700 so excessive height lost in emergency descent
- Not maintaining the correct glide speed
- Taking too long to pick a field in emergency and EFATO or picking an inappropriate field: too small, surrounded by trees and houses, gliding over a town, too high, not noticing pylons, and so on.

Fail points:

- No engine warming
- Not making the field as too high or too low, and doing nothing to correct it
- Wrong drill performed for the emergency stated
- Landing with a tailwind component unless the field chosen is sufficiently long to land safely in
- Doing the drill in a different and wrong order as stated in the checklist
- Too high and fast an approach, i.e. not maintaining the correct glide speed and misjudging the wind strength.

11 After the CPL...

Congratulations! You are now a commercial pilot and the envy of most people in the world. You should be feeling great. But (and there is always a but) there is still some way to go to be an airline pilot. The CPL really is only the beginning.

Firstly, think about getting your licence issued. Unless you are planning to get an MEP and IR in the near future and you want them issued at the same time, you should go to Gatwick as soon as possible with your logbook, the pass certificate, yet more money and get that licence issued. The CAA website will give the current licence-issue fees. Once they have processed your application and checked your hours and other details they will give you your shiny new EASA CPL licence in a blue plastic wallet (the ATPL licence comes in a green wallet).

If you don't get your CPL issued within 18 months, the pass becomes invalid and you will have to do the skills test again. It sounds like an obvious thing that you wouldn't forget to do, but I know of a student that it happened to. It cost him quite a lot of time and money to get back up to test standard, not to mention the test fee and aircraft hire...

It is good idea to take a few days off if you can and let it all sink in. It's a heck of a roller coaster of a ride to get this far and it's not uncommon for it to take days or even weeks to realize that you are now a commercial pilot licence holder. Then, as soon as you and your finances can cope, the next step is the multi-engine course and then an IR course.

With the IMEP and IR course done, you should get yourself onto a multi-crew cooperation course or even a Jet Orientation Course or a type rating if you have the time or any money left. There are various companies that offer MCC and/or JOC courses, some on expensive full-motion simulators and others on static simulators. Do your research, ask other pilots what

After the CPL...

Piper PA34 Seneca – the usual suspect in the multi engine rating.

Diamond DA42 Twinstar – the aircraft of choice for the IR. A truly lovely aeroplane to fly with a glass cockpit and FADEC.

training they did and where, and get a balanced view before making a decision. Some airlines want an MCC before you can even apply for a job, while others will give you one once you join; the key point here is that you want to keep the professional training going while you are still fresh in the mindset of flying like a professional. Like any other skill, flying talents that you now have will start to fade if you don't keep them current.

Don't forget that you can train to become a flying instructor. You will build hours and experience while looking for an airline job, and make yourself some great friends for life with your students and other instructors.

12 Privileges of a CPL

I've never known an industry that can get into people's blood the way aviation does.
Robert Six, founder of Continental Airlines

So, you have a EASA-FCL CPL (A) ... but what can you do with it? CAP 408 details the privileges of holding a CPL in full, but here I list the main points of what you can and can't do.

WHAT YOU CAN DO

The holder of a Commercial Pilot's Licence (Aeroplanes) is entitled to exercise the privileges of a United Kingdom Private Pilot's Licence (Aeroplanes), which includes an instrument meteorological conditions rating (aeroplane) and a night rating (aeroplanes) or night qualification.

The holder is entitled to fly as pilot in command of an aeroplane on a special VFR flight notwithstanding that the flight visibility is less than 3 km and when the aeroplane is taking off from or landing at any place notwithstanding that the flight visibility below cloud is less than 1,800m.

The holder is entitled to fly as pilot in command of an aeroplane of a type or class on which the holder is so qualified and which is specified in an aircraft rating included in the licence when the aeroplane is flying on a flight for any purpose whatsoever.

However, the holder is entitled to fly as pilot in command of an aeroplane of a type or class specified in an instructor's rating included in the licence on a flight for the purpose of aerial work which consists of instruction or testing in a club environment.

The holder may exercise the privileges specified above only in an aeroplane which the holder is entitled to fly as pilot in

Privileges of a CPL

command on a private flight, an aerial work flight, a public transport flight or a commercial air transport flight

The holder is entitled to fly as co-pilot of any aeroplane of a type specified in an aircraft rating included in the licence when the aeroplane is flying on a flight for any purpose of commercial air transport or public transport.

WHAT YOU CAN'T DO

The holder may *not* (unless the licence includes an instrument rating (aeroplane)) fly such an aeroplane on any scheduled journey; or fly as pilot in command of an aeroplane carrying passengers unless the holder has carried out at least three take-offs and three landings as pilot flying in an aeroplane of the same type or class or in a flight simulator, approved for the purpose of the aeroplane type or class to be used, in the preceding 90 days; or as co-pilot serve at the flying controls in an aeroplane carrying passengers during take-off and landing unless the holder has carried out at least three take-offs and three landings as pilot flying in an aeroplane of the same type or class or in a flight simulator, approved for the purpose of the aeroplane type or class to be used, in the preceding 90 days.

And, the holder may *not* if the licence does not include an instrument rating (aeroplane), fly as pilot in command of an aeroplane carrying passengers at night unless during the previous 90 days at least, one of the take-offs and landings required at night, unless the licence includes an instrument rating (aeroplane), fly any such aeroplane which has a maximum total weight authorised exceeding 2,300kg on any flight for the purpose of commercial air transport or public transport, except a flight beginning and ending at the same aerodrome and not extending beyond 25 nautical miles from that aerodrome; or fly such an aeroplane on a flight for the purpose of commercial air transport or public transport unless it is certified for single pilot operation; or fly such an aeroplane on any flight for the purpose of commercial air transport or public transport after attaining the age of 60 years unless the aeroplane is fitted with dual controls and carries a second pilot who has not attained the age of 60 years and who holds an appropriate licence under this Order entitling the second pilot to act as pilot in command or co-pilot of that aeroplane; or unless the licence includes an instrument rating (aeroplane), fly as pilot in command or co-pilot of such an aeroplane flying in Class A, B or C airspace in circumstances which require compliance with the instrument flight rules.

A final note: you must make yourselves aware of the new EASA rules and regulations covering you and your licence before you undertake any commercial flying work, as it's *your* responsibility. If in doubt, contact the CAA.

USEFUL INFORMATION

WEATHER

The Met office provide a telephone service on 0870 900 0100 (or 01392 885680). They are charged at the UK national call rate and are useful numbers to have stored somewhere in case you can't get access to the internet. They can give you TAFs, METARs, warnings, clarification of AIRMET regional forecasts as well as explanations of the Form 214 (spot winds) and Form 215 (area forecast).

Wind Component Table – Crosswind
Read off the crosswind in degrees between the wind direction and the runway heading against the wind strength:

Windspeed	10 deg	20 deg	30 deg	40 deg	50 deg	60 deg	70 deg	80 deg
5kt	1	2	2	3	4	4	4	5
10kt	2	3	5	6	7	8	9	9
15kt	3	5	7	9	11	13	14	14
20kt	3	7	10	13	15	17	18	19
25kt	4	8	12	16	19	22	23	24
30kt	5	10	15	19	23	28	28	29

Wind Component Table – Headwind
Read off the headwind in degrees between the wind direction and the runway heading against the wind strength:

Useful Information

Windspeed	Angle							
	10 deg	*20 deg*	*30 deg*	*40 deg*	*50 deg*	*60 deg*	*70 deg*	*80 deg*
5kt	5	4	4	4	3	2	2	1
10kt	9	9	8	7	6	5	3	2
15kt	14	14	13	11	9	7	5	3
20kt	19	18	17	15	13	10	7	3
25kt	24	23	22	19	16	12	8	4
30kt	29	28	26	23	19	15	10	5

MORSE CODE

A	Alpha	._
B	Bravo	_...
C	Charlie	_._.
D	Delta	_..
E	Echo	.
F	Foxtrot	.._.
G	Golf	_ _.
H	Hotel	....
I	India	..
J	Juliet	.___
K	Kilo	_._
L	Lima	._..
M	Mike	_ _
N	November	_.
O	Oscar	___
P	Papa	.__.
Q	Quebec	_ _._
R	Romeo	._.
S	Sierra	...
T	Tango	_
U	Uniform	.._
V	Victor	..._
W	Whiskey	.__
X	X ray	_.._
Y	Yankee	_.__
Z	Zulu	_ _..

CONVERSIONS

To Convert	Into	Multiply By
Celsius	Fahrenheit	1.8 and add 32
Fahrenheit	Celsius	Subtract 32 and multiply by 0.555
Centimetres	Inches	0.394
Feet	Metres	0.3048
Imp Gallons	US Gallons	1.2
Imp Gallons	Litres	4.546
Inches	Centimetres	2.540
Kilos	Pounds	2.2046
Kilometres	Nautical miles	0.539
Litres	Imp Gallons	0.220
Litres	US Gallons	0.264
Metres	Feet	3.281
Pounds	Kilograms	0.4536
Knots	MPH	1.1515
MPH	Knots	0.8684
Pounds	Kilos	0.4536
Miles	Nautical miles	0.8684
Nm	Kilometres	1.852
Nm	Metres	1852
US Gallons	Imp Gallons	0.833
US Gallons	Litres	3.79
Yards	Metres	0.914
Metres	Yards	1.094

107

Glossary of Terms & Abbreviations

A/P	Autopilot
Ab initio	No previous flying experience
ABCCD	Airfields, built up areas, cloud, controlled airspace, danger areas-part of location in the HASELL checks
ADF	Automatic Direction Finder
AH	Artificial Horizon
AI	Attitude Indicator
AME	Authorised Medical Examiner
AMSL	Above Mean Sea Level
ANO	Air Navigation Order
AoB	Angle of Bank
AOC	Air Operation Certificate
ARC	Airworthiness Review Certificate
ASI	Airspeed Indicator
ASR	Altimeter Setting Region
ASR	Altimeter Setting Region
ATA	Actual time of Arrival
ATC	Air Traffic Control
ATIS	Automatic Terminal Information Service
ATO	Air Training Organization
ATPL	Airline Transport Pilot Licence
ATSU	Air Traffic Service Unit
ATZ	Aerodrome Traffic Zone
CAA	Civil Aviation Authority
CAP413	R/T Procedures – EASA
CAP804	Flight Crew Licensing – EASA
CAVOK	Ceiling and Visibility OK
CDI	Course Deviation Indicator
Check A	First and arguably the most important check of the aircraft
CoG	Centre of Gravity
Comm 1	Communication unit 1: for entering frequencies for transmission
Comm 2	Communication unit 2: for entering frequencies for transmission

COR	Certificate of Release to Service
CPL(A)	Commercial Pilot Licence Aeroplane
CRM	Crew Resource Management
CRP	CRP-5, Slide Rule for Calculations
DI	Direction Indicator
DME	Distance Measuring Equipment
DOC	Designated area of Operational Coverage
DRAAG	Diversion Checks – Danger areas, Restricted areas, Airspace, Airfields, Glider sites
EASA	European Aviation Safety Agency
EFATO	Engine Failure After Take Off
ETA	Estimated Time of Arrival
FAA	Federal Aviation Authority
fATPL	Frozen ATPL
FI	Fling Instructor
FIR	Flight Information Region
Fpm	Feet per minute
FREDA	Cruise Checks – Fuel, Radio, Engine, Direction, Altitude
GMT	Greenwich Mean Time
GPS	Global Positioning System
HASELL	Stalling Checks – Height, Airframe, Security, Engine, Location, Lookout
HDG	Heading
HELL	Abbreviated HASELL Checks – Height, Engine, Location, Lookout
HSI	Horizontal Situation Indicator
hPa	hectopascals
IAS	Indicated Air Speed
ICAO	International Civil Aviation Organization
IF	Instrument Flying
IFR	Instrument Flight Rules
ILS	Instrument Landing System
IMC	Instrument Meteorological Conditions
IR	Instrument Rating
ISA	International Standard Atmosphere
JAA	Joint Aviation Authority
JAR-FCL	Joint Aviation Requirements – Flight Crew Licensing (replaced with Part FCL under EASA)
JOC	Jet Orientation Course

kt	Knots
LARS	Lower Airspace Radar Service
LASORS	Licensing Administration Standardisation Operating Requirements Safety – replaced by CAP 804 under EASA
LDA	Landing Distance Available
LDR	Landing Distance Required
mb	Millibar
MCC	Multi-Crew Co-operation Course
MCL	Multi-Crew Licence
MEL	Minimum Equipment List
MEP	Multi-Engine Piston
METAR	Actual Weather Report
MP	Manifold Pressure
MPL	Multi-Pilots Licence
MR	Multi-Rating
MSA	Minimum Safety Altitude
Nav	Navigation – cross country navigation lesson
Nav. 1	Navigation unit 1: for entering frequencies for navigation aids
Nav. 2	Navigation unit 2: for entering frequencies for navigation aids
NDB	Non Directional Beacon
Nm	Nautical mile
NOTAMS	Notice to Airmen
OAT	Outside Air Temperature
OBS	Omni Directional Bearing Selector
PAPI	Precision Approach Position Indicator
Pax	Passengers
PFL	Practice Forced Landing
PIC	Pilot in Command
Plog	Pilot's Log - completed on navigation exercises
POH	Pilot Operating Handbook
PPL	Private Pilot Licence
PTT	Press to Transmit switch
PUT	Pilot Under Training – CPL flying training
QDM	Magnetic bearing to a station
QDR	Magnetic bearing from a station
QFE	Height above ground level pressure setting

Glossary of Terms & Abbreviations

QNH	Altitude above sea level pressure setting
QRH	Quick Reference Handbook
R/T	Radio Telephony
RBI	Relative Bearing Indicator
RMI	Radio Magnetic Indicator
ROC	Rate of Climb
ROD	Rate of Descent
rpm	Revolutions per Minute
SEP	Single Engine Piston
SOP	Standard Operating Procedures
SSR	Secondary Surveillance Radar
TACAN	Military Beacons with DME and bearing information
TAF	Terminal Area Forecast
TAS	True Airspeed
TMA	Terminal Manoeuvering Area
TODA	Take-Off Distance Available
TOGA	Take-Off/Go-Around
TORA	Take-Off Runway Available
TORR	Take-Off Runway Required
UTC	Universal Co-Ordinated Time (Greenwich Mean Time)
Va	Maximum Manoeuvring Speed
VDF	VHF Direction Finding
VFR	Visual Flight Rules
VMC	Visual Meteorological Conditions
VOLMET	Spoken list of airfield METARs
VOR	VHF Omni Directional Radio Range
Vref	Minimum Speed over the Threshold
VRP	Visual Reference Point
VSI	Vertical Speed Indicator
Vx	Best Angle of Climb Speed
Vy	Best Rate of Climb Speed
Wx	Weather
ZULU	Greenwich Mean Time

INDEX

170A and Skill Test:
   briefing by examiner 91
   conduct of test 92
   preparation for 88
   tolerances 94

acceleration and deceleration 43, 54
Air Training Organisations 15

bad weather circuits 38
base to final approach stall 48
brake checks 30

captain's brief 29
catastrophic engine failure in the air 78
circuits 34–43
clean stall 47
climbing and descending 45, 54
CPL course:
   requirements to start 20
   course content 21
cross wind technique 42

diversion planning 71
diversion checks 74

emergencies 77–85
engine failure after take-off 84
engine fire in the air 78

final approach stall 49
flapless approach 36
flight instrument/internal checks 26

general airwork 43–50
glide approach 37
go-around 39
ground checks 26

HASELL Checks 46
hour building 13

instrument flying 51–63
insurance 88
integrated training 18

limited panel – scan 55
limited panel – timed turns 55
limited panel – unusual attitude recoveries 57

maintenance 24
medium and steep turns 44
modular training 18

navigation 64–76
NDB Tracking 60
normal approach 35

passengers 29
planning a diversion route 71
planning a navigation route 64
position fix 54
power checks 32

radio/navigation aid instrument checks 59
rejected take off 39
re-startable engine failure in the air 78
runway checks 33

stalls 46
steep gliding turns 45

taxying 30
technical log 24
track correction method 70
turning/instrument checks 31
turns 54

visual unusual attitude recoveries 44
VOR Tracking 62

weight and balance 88

112